Cambridge Elements ≡

Elements in Environmental Humanities
edited by
Louise Westling
University of Oregon
Serenella Iovino
University of North Carolina at Chapel Hill
Timo Maran
University of Tartu

THE OPEN VEINS
OF MODERNITY

Ecological Crisis and the Legacy of Byzantium and Pre-Columbian America

Eleni Kefala
University of St Andrews

CAMBRIDGE
UNIVERSITY PRESS

Shaftesbury Road, Cambridge CB2 8EA, United Kingdom

One Liberty Plaza, 20th Floor, New York, NY 10006, USA

477 Williamstown Road, Port Melbourne, VIC 3207, Australia

314–321, 3rd Floor, Plot 3, Splendor Forum, Jasola District Centre, New Delhi – 110025, India

103 Penang Road, #05–06/07, Visioncrest Commercial, Singapore 238467

Cambridge University Press is part of Cambridge University Press & Assessment, a department of the University of Cambridge.

We share the University's mission to contribute to society through the pursuit of education, learning and research at the highest international levels of excellence.

www.cambridge.org
Information on this title: www.cambridge.org/9781009547116

DOI: 10.1017/9781009547079

When citing this work, please include a reference to the DOI 10.1017/9781009547079

First published 2024

A catalogue record for this publication is available from the British Library

ISBN 978-1-009-54711-6 Hardback
ISBN 978-1-009-54710-9 Paperback
ISSN 2632-3125 (online)
ISSN 2632-3117 (print)

The Open Veins of Modernity

Ecological Crisis and the Legacy of Byzantium and Pre-Columbian America

Elements in Environmental Humanities

DOI: 10.1017/9781009547079
First published online: December 2024

Eleni Kefala
University of St Andrews

Author for correspondence: Eleni Kefala, ek30@st-andrews.ac.uk

Abstract: The ecological crisis is the result of modernity's coloniality. The Moderns considered the Earth as "natural resources" at their disposal. Their colonial vision of nature was complemented by that of nonmodern cultures like Byzantium and pre-Columbian America as passive or primitive, respectively. For the Moderns, the Byzantines were the "librarians of humanity," an inert repository of Greco-Roman knowledge, unable to produce their own. Byzantium's inertia was matched by that of nature, both reservoirs of epistemic and material resources. Thanks to those "librarians," the supposedly inexhaustible supply of natural resources, and the epistemic and material riches of indigenous America, the Moderns believed they were inaugurating an epoch of intellectual maturity and infinite growth. Today, the enduring negative view of Byzantium and the ecological crisis confirm that we remain entangled in modernity's coloniality. We should decolonize both history and nature. To mitigate humanity's existential threat, modernity must be rethought and overcome.

Keywords: ecological crisis, modernity, Byzantium, pre-Columbian America, decolonization

ISBNs: 9781009547116 (HB), 9781009547109 (PB), 9781009547079 (OC)
ISSNs: 2632-3125 (online), 2632-3117 (print)

Contents

Parode: The Leaky Jar of the Modern

What do Byzantium and pre-Columbian America have to do with the ecological crisis? This Element argues that if Byzantium and America are siblings, in the sense that they were both inferiorized by European modernity and became unlikely partners in its rise and consolidation, colonized nature is their close relative. The coloniality of human others is interwoven with the coloniality of the Earth's environment and nonhuman living beings. "Human resources" and "natural resources" are two notions at the heart of the crisis of modernity from which we should exit, hence the title of the Element: *The Open Veins of Modernity.*[1] The intimate link between colonized histories and colonized nature stresses the need to move beyond the colonial vision of modernity and reminds us that environmental humanities holds center stage in the battle against climate change. Therefore, this Element's purpose is twofold. On the one hand, it aims to explain why Byzantium matters to ecology, arguing that decolonizing modernity's abiding view of Byzantium is akin to decolonizing modernity's view of nature. The imperative to decolonize both history and nature, on the other, leads to the Element's second purpose, which is to advocate for the necessity to step beyond modernity. If we are to curb the ecological crisis, we must leave modernity. But what do we mean by "modernity"?

The concept of "modernity" is ambivalent and elusive with regards both to its origins and meanings. As a notion, it is closely related to the terms "modern" and "progress." The earliest use of the word "modern," in Latin *modernus*, dates to the late fifth century and is found in the letters of Pope Gelasius I where it is used to distinguish contemporary events from the early Christian era. *Modernus*, meaning both "new" and "of that time," stood for the pope's age (what he called "our age" or *nostra aetas*) against the antiquity (*antiquitas*) of the fathers of the Church. The modern is always displaced by itself, the *just newer*; in other words, it is constantly splitting from itself (the newer separates itself from the new) and on that account every modernity is inevitably destined to become antiquity (Jauss 2005: 333, 363). We could read the history of modernity since the European Enlightenment in the late seventeenth and eighteenth centuries as a period fixated with the idea of the "new" and the idea progress, two terms that largely overlap in modernity's lexicon. As a historical stage, modernity has turned the concepts of innovation and progress into a fetish.

To put it differently, ever since the Enlightenment, modernity and progress have shared the same berth on the wagon of history; the rhetoric of progress is simultaneously the rhetoric of modernity. Warren Wagar traces the modern idea of progress in the French philosopher Jean Bodin's attack on the myth of the

---

[1] The Element's title is inspired by Eduardo Galeano's *Open Veins of Latin America* (1971).

Golden Age (Wagar 1969: 41), that is, the idea that better times lay in the past and that the present is the result of some kind of temporal decline. "They who say that all things were understood by the ancients," writes Bodin in 1565, "err not less than do those who deny them the early conquest of many arts." But Bodin's notion of history, and of many others in the next hundred years, remains cyclical, as he concludes that "the path of change seems to go in a circle" (Bodin 1945: 302). Drawing on the accomplishments of modern science, Bernard Le Bovier de Fontenelle breaks with cyclicism and instead envisions history as marching forward on the trail of progress. In his "Digression on the Ancients and the Moderns" (1688), he argues that "enlightened by the views of the ancients, and even by their faults, we not surprisingly surpassed them" (Fontenelle 1969: 53–54). Crucially, Fontenelle is not professing progress in the spheres of art and morality. As a forerunner of the Enlightenment, he stays faithful to the idea of scientific and philosophical advancement. Meanwhile, his contemporary Gottfried Wilhelm Leibniz applies the concept of continuous progress to the universe, which, like the human spirit, "could never reach a last degree of maturity. As a whole, the universe never slipped backwards nor aged" (Koselleck 2002: 227; Wagar 1969: 48).

About a century after Fontenelle, Kant will formulate the now classical notion of universal progress at regular intervals. In his "Idea for a Universal History from a Cosmopolitan Point of View" (1784), the German philosopher postulates that "when the play of the freedom of the human Will is examined on the great scale of universal history, a regular march will be discovered in its movements." Kant sees the "history of the whole species as a continually advancing, though slow, development of its original capacities and endow-ments," and advocates that the progression of universal history from "the rudeness of barbarism to the culture of civilisation" is "no doubt to a certain extent of an *a priori* character." It is the result of a "universal plan in Nature," which drives humanity, teleologically, through "the progress of enlightenment" to its full growth (Kant 1891: 3, 10–11, 27–28). In the same year, Kant publishes his essay "An Answer to the Question: 'What is Enlightenment'" where he famously associates Enlightenment and progress with maturity. Enlightenment, he claims, is "man's emergence from his self-incurred immaturity," which he defines as "the inability to use one's own understanding without the guidance of another." For Kant, non-enlightened societies are coward and lazy; they need to "gradually work their way out of barbarism." Our age, he confesses, may not be enlightened, "but we do live in an age of enlightenment." Although not all people use "their own understanding confidently and well in religious matters, without outside guidance [,] [. . .] the way is now being cleared for them to work freely in this direction." Kant concludes that the barriers to universal enlightenment, in other words, to our self-inflicted immaturity, are steadily diminishing (Kant 1991: 54, 58–59).

But the question remains as to what we mean by "modernity." The term has been used to refer, among others, to the Italian Renaissance and the conquest of America by the Spaniards and Portuguese, often called *early* or *first* modernity, Descartes, the Enlightenment, the French Revolution, and the Industrial Revolution that led to the second wave of North European colonialism from the second half of the eighteenth to the early twentieth centuries, sometimes called *second* modernity, and, of course, the emergence of capitalism (Dussel 2002: 227–228; Escobar 2003: 60; Jameson 2002: 31–32; Karkov and Robbins 2014: 6).[2] The literature on the issue is abundant, but despite the lack of agreement, René Descartes's *cogito* ("I think, therefore I am" or "I am thinking, therefore I exist"), first put forward in *A Discourse on the Method* (1637), has often been taken as the beginning of modernity (Descartes 2006: 28). If first modernity exemplified the coloniality of other human beings (those non-Europeans who were often thought of as "savage" or "primitive" and those pre-Moderns whose histories, we shall see, were described by the Italian Renaissance as "dark" and "retrograde"), Descartes's split of the subject from the object, the mind from the body/nature (*res cogitans*, or "thinking thing" / *res extensa*, or "extended thing") inaugurated second modernity's "coloniality of nature," a term I borrow from decolonial thinkers like Nelson Maldonado-Torres, Arturo Escobar, and Catherine Walsh, among others (Descartes 2008: 15, 19, 32; Escobar 2011; Maldonado-Torres 2007: 135; Walsh 2012: 68).[3] For Descartes's thinking subject ("I think"), nature becomes natural resources at humanity's disposal, which suggests that climate crisis is essentially born with modernity. Conceived with the Cartesian dualism of mind-body and nurtured by

---

[2] Fredric Jameson also mentions the Protestant Reformation, Galileo, and the "Nietzschean death of God," among others (Jameson 2002: 31–32).

[3] See also Lander (2002), Escobar (2005), and Alimonda (2011). According to Latin American decolonial thinking, colonialism is a historical manifestation of coloniality, the latter being a pattern of power that persists in global capitalism. Maldonado-Torres refers to the "coloniality of being" as the ontological aspect of what Aníbal Quijano called "coloniality of power," which alludes to a hegemonic power model based on the purported superiority of Europe over non-European cultures. The term "coloniality of being" was first used by Walter Mignolo (Kefala 2011: 1, 3–4, 16–17; Maldonado-Torres 2007: 146–147; Mignolo 2001: 30–48; Quijano 2000). My use of the term "coloniality of human others" is akin to that of "coloniality of being." Maldonado-Torres defines coloniality as "discourse and practice," which advocates both "the natural inferiority of subjects and the colonization of nature," identifying "certain subjects as dispensable and nature as pure raw material for the production of goods in the international market" (Maldonado-Torres 2007: 135). Walsh reminds us that the "coloniality of nature" is intertwined with the "coloniality of power," "coloniality of being," and "coloniality of knowledge," acknowledging that the coloniality of "Mother Nature [...] finds its basis in the binary nature/society" (Walsh 2012: 67–68). On the notion "coloniality of knowledge," see Lander (2000).

the Enlightenment idea of linear, unbounded progress, modernity appears to have been rushing headlong to an unpredictable future with far-reaching consequences. "Cheap nature is at an end," says Donna Haraway, citing Jason Moore. Earth's reserves have been "drained, burned, depleted, poisoned, exterminated, and otherwise exhausted" (Haraway 2016: 100).

Meanwhile, European colonialism reveals the "darker side" or "underside" of *ego cogito*, which is *ego conquiro*, or "I conquer." "If the *ego cogito* was formulated and acquired practical relevance on the basis of *ego conquiro*," writes Maldonado-Torres, "this means that 'I think, therefore I am' has at least two unforeseen dimensions. Beneath 'I think' we could read 'they do not think', and inside 'I am', we could trace the philosophical justification for the idea that 'others are not'" (Dussel 1996; Maldonado-Torres 2007: 144; Mignolo 1995). The idea that "Others do not think, therefore they are not," implicit in the Cartesian *cogito*, explains philosophically the Europeans' doubt as regards the humanity of the others or their state of "progress," and justifies, in their eyes, their colonization and racialization. *Ego conquiro* constitutes the darker side of modernity, which is manifested in the dominion and control of other human beings and their histories, as well as nature (Kefala 2011: 16; Maldonado-Torres 2007: 144–145). In short, in the Cartesian *cogito* there is reflected a double coloniality: the coloniality of human others and the coloniality of nature and nonhuman living beings, which David Abram has called the "more-than-human world" (Abram 1996).

Clearly, no other historical period has ever been so wrapped up in the idea of progress than modernity, for which the words "modern" and "progressive" are synonymous. If "modern" retains currency today, it is because of this conceptual overlap with progress. Even if their mutual dependency has repeatedly and fiercely come under attack following two world wars, the Holocaust, chemical and biological warfare, the freshly resurrected threat of nuclear catastrophe, and the ecological crisis, the consensus appears to live on in our collective consciousness largely unbothered. Far from being surpassed, "modern," "modernity," and along with them "progress" are now classics. This we could call the paradox of the modern – it is an ancient yet youthful concept. Like Hebe, the Greek goddess of youth, the modern promises eternal newness through the nectar of rationalism and the ambrosia of progress. But we know that the jar of the modern is leaking. Like the forty-nine daughters of Danaus, who day after day poured water into a perforated jug, several generations of thinkers have been tirelessly filling it with theories, yet neither its origins nor its evolution are free of controversy, while its meaning remains as elusive as ever. A catch-all word, the modern seems to be suitable for any occasion and purpose.

Let us imagine ourselves for a moment in the amphitheater. We are watching the drama of modernity. The Danaids are the chorus of fated nymphs who have entered the orchestra wailing; we see them filling the leaky jar of the modern. The Element consists of a "Parode," two "Episodes," and an "Exodus," which are terms I borrow from ancient Greek drama. "Parode" and "Exodus" referred to the entrance and exit songs of the chorus before and after the first and final episodes of the play. In this Element, whose reading time will not exceed that of a Greek play, "Parode: The Leaky Jar of the Modern" will be followed by "Episode One: Coloniality of Human Others." Here I will discuss the alleged exceptionalism or superiority of modernity over other cultures across time and space with a focus on Byzantium and pre-Columbian America. I will argue that modernity's supposed superiority over premodern and nonmodern cultures, what the decolonial philosopher Enrique Dussel has called "the irrational myth of modernity" (Dussel 1996: 52), goes hand in hand with the assumed inferiority of endogenous (European) and exogenous (non-European) histories. The Moderns viewed what was external to them temporally and spatially as static, retrograde, or simply inferior. I call *endogenous inferiorization* the case of the Middle Ages, a period condemned by the early Moderns as dark and regressive, while with *exogenous inferiorization* I refer to European colonialism during first and second modernity. Christopher Columbus's arrival in the Caribbean on October 12, 1492, paved the way for the colonization of America and the rise of western modernity, which saw non-European cultures as regressive or immature (Kefala 2020: 11–14).

With the role of pre-Columbian America in the rise of western modernity by now substantially revised, the contribution of Greco-Roman antiquity long recognized, the part played by Islamic culture duly acknowledged, and that of the western Middle Ages gradually reinstated, the imagery of darkness, regressiveness, and passivity has been kept largely for Byzantium. Perceived by the Moderns as an epistemic backwater, the eleven-century-long Byzantine Empire (330–1453), which saw itself as the heir of Greco-Roman antiquity and a continuation of the Roman Empire (hence, it is also referred to as "Eastern Roman Empire"), exemplifies what I call "the irrational myth of modernity at home." We often tend to forget that the Moderns established their exceptionalism at home before setting sail for abroad. Preconquest America epitomizes "the irrational myth of modernity abroad" (Kefala 2020: 13–14). Although the Enlightenment enterprise overseas has generally ceased to be viewed as a civilizing force, coloniality at home has partially gone unnoticed, often even within postcolonial and decolonial studies. We will see that Edward Said's gaze is orientalist. He understands Byzantium as static or inert, passively mediating between the "dead people" of antiquity and the Italian Renaissance (Said 1994: 195), while Dussel disregards Byzantium's ability to directly impart its heritage, which contributed to the rise of the Italian Renaissance and the western revival of ancient knowledge.

What Byzantium tells us is that, for all our conscientious efforts, the colonial gaze of the Enlightenment looms large. We still need to pull off the veil of the discursive mechanisms which have allowed the Moderns to label one of the world's most enduring civilizations, with important epistemic accomplishments in many spheres of life, as inert or even regressive. Byzantium and pre-Columbian America are clearly not the only civilizations with epistemic achievements on the cusp of modernity. The examples of China and the Islamic world, which among many others led to the emergence of western modernity, are telling. Of course, we all know that premodern societies engaged in imperialism, slavery, exploitation, religious bigotry, patriarchy, and in some cases human sacrifice. Are we contrasting our lives today to those of the Byzantines and Aztecs (who called themselves "Romans" and "Mexica," respectively), most of them doomed to eke out a living from strenuous agricultural work, and concluding that it was better then than now? Certainly not! A critical reading of modernity *does not refute the very real and often spectacular advances ushered in, thick and fast, by the Moderns in so many realms of our life.* Who would like to endure the Plague of Athens that ravaged the ancient city-state and even claimed the life of its famous leader, Pericles, or live through the Justinianic Plague that not even Emperor Justinian himself could avoid, not to mention Black Death, the deadliest pandemic ever documented, and the Cocoliztli Epidemic, which wiped out millions of indigenous peoples in sixteenth-century Mexico? Acknowledging that progress, however one defines the term, has never been a monopoly of a handful of countries west of Jerusalem is neither romantic primitivism nor nostalgia for a return to a premodern Eden. Nor does it imply that had one of those alternative historical paths prevailed over European modernity today we would be living in a global eutopia, a pleasant and joyful place. It also does not suggest that such paths were free of contradictions, misjudgments, and inherent flaws. But it does cast serious doubt on the Moderns' fixation with the idea of progress, the latent assumption that innovation was either limited or generally unwanted outside modernity's historical and conceptual frame of reference, and on the exceptionalism of western modernity, especially when seen through the lens of the current ecological crisis. Climate change questions modernity's narrative of safety and security, which is one of the dimensions of progress as defined by Jürgen Habermas – "well-being and security, freedom and dignity, happiness and fulfillment" (Habermas 1979: 164).[4] Similarly, if the COVID-19 pandemic has reminded us of modern science's remarkable achievements (consider the unprecedented production of life-saving vaccines

---

[4] On Habermas's idea of progress, see Owen (2002).

and antiviral drugs in record time), it has also shown us how vulnerable and insecure our enlightened humanity is.

We know that "progress" is not one-sided, or monolectic, but rather double-edged and riddled with contradictions. We have been aware of this at least since Marx's time. "The new-fangled sources of wealth," Marx famously said in 1856, "by some strange weird spell, are turned into sources of want. [...] All our invention and progress seem to result in endowing material forces with intellectual life, and in stultifying human life into a material force" (Marx and Engels 1980: 655–656). The controversy surrounding progress is not just owed to its dialectic nature. Strong supporters of the idea, both Ancients and Moderns, have clearly wrestled with the notion of linear progress in domains other than science and technology, such as the moral and artistic spheres. However, there is widespread agreement that science and technology are the two areas where modern progress is most visible, a view that is barely new. Throughout Greco-Roman antiquity, the most explicit affirmations of the notion concern scientific progress and are made by active scientists or authors dealing with scientific topics (Dodds 1973: 24).

Science and technology seem to make progress measurable, but even here the modern account of progress does not stand free of controversy. There is no doubt that modern science and technology, and the new landscapes they have produced, have been spectacular but, to use Bernard de Chartres's famous metaphor of dwarfs standing on the shoulders of giants (*nani gigantum humeris insidentes*), the spectacle most likely would have been suspended had it not been for those giants on whose shoulders the actors of modernity ultimately stood. "In the infancy of the world," Fontenelle admits, "all that Archimedes could have done would have been to invent the plow," and the same may be said of the birth of modernity (Fontenelle 1969: 52; Jauss 2005: 336; Sarewitz 2013: 303). In this light, the opposition between past/slow and modern/fast progress hardly infers a superiority of the modern over premodern or nonmodern histories. It is in this context that Bruno Latour questions the exceptionalism of modernity. "*In potentia* the modern world is a total and irreversible invention that breaks with the past," he argues, "just as *in potentia* the French or Bolshevik Revolutions were midwives at the birth of a new world." But when regarded as networks, he adds, the modern world allows for little more than short expansions of existing practices and societies, modest accelerations in the flow of knowledge, a minor rise in the number of actors, and slight adjustments to previous beliefs. Viewed as networks, "Western innovations remain recognizable and important, but they no longer suffice as the stuff of saga, a vast saga of radical rupture, fatal destiny, irreversible good or bad fortune" (Latour 1993: 48).

As modernity's coloniality of other humans and their histories across time and space is matched by the coloniality of the more-than-human world (the non-living and other-than-human living beings), the modern image of Byzantium as passive becomes intriguingly relevant to our critical discussions of the ecological crisis today. The Moderns, I will argue, saw Byzantium and nature as inert and as repositories of epistemic and material resources from which they could draw freely. This is why Byzantium matters to ecology. In our collective struggle to survive on this aching planet, we need to deliver ourselves from the fixations of the Enlightenment that have colonized nature and civilizations like Byzantium. "Episode Two: Coloniality of Nature" links modernity's coloniality of Byzantium and America to the coloniality of nature and the concomitant ecological crisis, whose birth it traces in the seventeenth century and more specifically in the natural philosophy of Francis Bacon and Descartes's subjectivity. This episode discusses the different ramifications of climate change, a "high-consequence risk of modernity" (Giddens 1991: 171) now turned into humanity's existential crisis, and the limitations of the term "Anthropocene" when seen from a postcolonial and decolonial point of view. As we are finally waking up, at least in theory, to the harsh realities of the ecological crisis, we appreciate that economic progress, growth, or development cannot be limitless. Is our modernity's newness new enough to break free from its past and current bankruptcies? Is it Hebe who waits in the mirror or Dorian Gray?

One could only speculate on the future ramifications of the current era, which has not yet rid itself of modernity's fixations and therefore does not yet constitute a real *post*-modernity. It is for this reason that, despite my previous use of the term "postmodernity," here I borrow Anthony Giddens's "high modernity" to refer to our contemporary situation (Giddens 1991: 163, 176; Kefala 2006). This shift in terminology involves a change in focus, not in content. While both "postmodernity" and "high modernity" are used with reference to our time, the latter term underscores the continuities rather than the discontinuities between the modern and the contemporary and in doing so it stresses the need to move beyond modernity.

"Exodus: Beyond Modernity" speaks of the necessity for a paradigm shift similar to the one experienced with the advent of modern subjectivity in the seventeenth century. Notions like cosmocentrism (Varese 2011), cosmocentric economy (Apffel-Marglin 2012), ecosystem stewardship (Chapin et al. 2011; Krupnik et al. 2018), and kincentric ecology (Martinez 2018; Salmon 2000) coming from indigenous knowledge systems or Traditional Ecological Knowledge (TEK) invite us to consider other ways of thinking about the Earth that are considerably different from the existing capitalist methods of resource extraction and exploitation. Such knowledge systems may not be sufficient to halt climate change, but they could aid in decolonizing our epistemic systems and replacing the "monoculture of scientific knowledge" with an "ecology of knowledges." In other words, they could help us rethink how modern scientific knowledge interacts with other knowledge systems (Sousa Santos et al. 2008: xx).

I argue that if we were to mitigate humanity's greatest crisis, we would need to step past modernity's reifying logic, which has turned nature and humanity into natural and human "resources." A true *post*-modern shift is required, one that would take us beyond the economy of modernity to what I call postmodern *ecologics* (from *economics* and *ecology*), forcing us to reconfigure the ways in which we administer our *oikos*. As already noted, I borrow the term "exodus" from Greek theater, where it meant the exit song of the chorus after the play's final episode. Like any other historical period, modernity, at once comic and tragic, joyous and bleak, is laden with contradictions. If, as the great dramatists William Shakespeare and Pedro Calderón de la Barca suggested, all the world is a theater, modernity may be the final episode of a drama from which we now need to exit (Calderón de la Barca 2005; Shakespeare 2004: 83). We, the modern Danaids, should finally be able to take a break from filling the leaky jar of the modern. Now more than ever, we must forge ahead and beyond fossilized views of the past, the present, and the future. We must exit modernity.

Episode One: Coloniality of Human Others

Historically, modernity's superiority has been argued for either as a break with the past or as its coming of age. The former can be observed in the Renaissance's characterization of the Middle Ages as the abyss of darkness – around 1381 Filippo Villani congratulated Dante for rescuing poetry *ex abysso tenebrarum* (Jauss 2005: 340; Villani 1847: 8). The latter is the time of second modernity, that is, of the Enlightenment and particularly Kant's notion of maturity. But whereas first modernity's break with the immediate past, the Middle Ages, was accompanied by the espousal of the Greco-Roman antiquity, second modernity's embrace of previous historical eras as distinct stages in the lifecycle of humanity (a gesture necessitated by the idea of universal progress and of modernity as humanity's adulthood) ultimately proved to be a mighty assault of the modern on the rest of time.[5] Ironically, the Enlightenment discourse of continuity was a more radical rupture with tradition (now regarded childish) than Renaissance's rejection of the Middle Ages, which was offset by its admiration of antiquity. By the eighteenth century, modernity is judged to be superior to the rest of history.

---

[5] Here I paraphrase Alexander Kluge's 1985 film, *The Assault of the Present on the Rest of Time*.

Modernity's alleged superiority is paired with the perceived inferiority of endogenous and exogenous histories. The Moderns saw what was external in time (Middle Ages) and space (non-European *oikoumenai*, or inhabited worlds) as dark and retrograde. Endogenous inferiorization is reflected in Villani's condemnation of the Middle Ages. We know that in its unyielding humanism and anthropocentrism, incipient modernity viewed the Middle Ages in negative light. Writing about medieval art, Panayotis Michelis points out that "the fanaticism of the humanistic mentality" that dominated the west since the Renaissance denounced the Middle Ages as a dark age marked by a barren artistic landscape (Michelis 1955: 3). But the Middle Ages were gradually reinstated, to some extent at least, by second modernity's historical revisionism that culminated in the nineteenth century in Romanticism's idealization of medieval culture. This is because the contrast between medieval darkness and classical (Greco-Roman) light, says Jochen Schlobach, offered a difficulty for the philosophers of the Enlightenment and proponents of universal progress; it appeared to demonstrate that historical regression was indeed possible. While early modernity criticized the Middle Ages "on aesthetic grounds, for their lack of good taste," the eighteenth-century Enlightenment saw the Middle Ages as an age of bigotry and ignorance. In his "Digression," notes Schlobach, Fontenelle had already admitted that it would be hard to apply the novel concept of progress to the medieval period. To explain this apparent regression, Fontenelle famously compared the medieval period, which he called "siècles barbares," or barbarous ages, to an illness or short-term amnesia, which "did not prevent the convalescent from resuming his education at the point where it had been interrupted." Others resorted to the trope of the underground river. In his *Studies on the Causes of Progress and Decadence in the Sciences and Arts* (1748), Anne-Robert-Jacques Turgot likened the medieval period to "those rivers that flow underground for part of their course but reappear further along, swollen with large quantity of water that has been filtered through the ground," paving the way for the gradual rehabilitation of the Middle Ages. Such images, argues Schlobach, show how challenging it was to integrate a condemnation of the medieval period into the Moderns' progressivist concept of history, which is why their work included a careful restoration of the Middle Ages. Among the examples he cites are Fontenelle, who praised medieval troubadour poetry a long time before the Romantics did, and the remarkable success of James Macpherson's *Poems of Ossian* (1765), which led to the partial restoration of the medieval period in the second half of the eighteenth century. In France, Comte de Tressan's adaptations of medieval romances had a comparable regenerating effect. The recovery of medieval culture, Schlobach concludes, laid the groundwork for Romanticism's admiration of medieval culture, which was now viewed as an essential component of the modern period (Fontenelle 1707: 119; Schlobach 2013: 67–68; Turgot 2018: 125–126). Eventually, the seeds of modernity were discovered in the so-called three medieval renaissances of western Europe – the Carolingian (late eighth–ninth centuries), the Ottonian (tenth century), and, especially, the twelfth-century humanist Renaissance.

Exogenous inferiorization is exemplified by historical colonialism, initially Spanish and Portuguese, and then English, French, and Dutch. For Columbus, the indigenous people lacked religion and should make "good servants," while early Spanish chroniclers present them as primitive, childish, and backward. Sixteenth-century French writers similarly see them as bereft of civility (Columbus 1969: 56; Jaenen 1982: 46). A century later, Fontenelle notes that "the barbarians of America" were "quite a young people when they were discovered by the Spaniards" (Fontenelle 1972: 16). These stereotypes lived on into the Enlightenment. Denis Diderot tells of a continent populated by primitives, "the most part still ferocious and who eat human flesh,"[6] Buffon writes of savages driven by the forces of nature, considering them as "almost inert peoples in terms of dominating their environment" and unable to develop materially and culturally (with the exception of Peru and Mexico), while Voltaire thinks of the history of peoples like the Caribs and Iroquois as "not worth writing" (Boucher 1992: 123; Jaenen 1982: 47, 49). Apart from the Peruvians who found in the Sun the supreme deity, in Voltaire's eyes the peoples of America did not possess "cultivated reason." His conclusion is that "reasoned knowledge," which he associates with the knowledge of a "creator God," "was absolutely lacking in all America" (Voltaire 2013: 212–213). Similarly, in his *Natural History*, Buffon sees the entire stretch of North America, from the Gulf of Mexico to the extreme north, as populated by people who are "stupid, ignorant, unacquainted with the arts, and destitute of industry," and attributes the "want of civilization" to the sparsity of population. But "if in North America there were none but savages," he writes, "in Mexico and Peru we found a polished people, subjected to laws, governed by kings, industrious, acquainted with the arts, and not destitute of religion." Even so, he concludes that the Americans are a "new people," judging from "their ignorance, and the little progress the most civilized among them had made in the arts" (Buffon 1797: 311–312, 315, 333).

The theme of the ignoble savage coexisted alongside that of the noble savage from early on, as shown in French concepts spanning from the sixteenth to the eighteenth centuries. The positive portrayal of indigenous peoples seen in the works of François Rabelais, Michel de Montaigne, and Pierre de Ronsard,

---

[6] The phrase appears in Diderot's *Encyclopedie* under the entry "Sauvage" (Diderot 1779: 188).

writes Cornelius Jaenen, was as old as their negative image, while conflicting views of them as childlike or degenerate continued throughout. The debate whether the indigenous were degenerated people or in the infancy of humanity persisted into the eighteenth century between, on the one hand, the champions of human perfectibility and the idea of progress and, on the other, those advocating the degeneracy of the Americas and the ageing of the world (Jaenen 1982: 46, 49). Philip Boucher cites Jean-Jacques Rousseau, Jean-Baptiste Labat, Joseph Lafitau, and Guillaume-Thomas Raynal as examples of eighteenth-century intellectuals who maintained the generally favorable views of seventeenth-century authors like Jean-Baptiste du Tertre and Charles de Rochefort but adds that prominent French philosophers vehemently opposed Rousseau's theory of natural man in order to defend their convictions about social progress. He calls Voltaire "perhaps the most disdainful of Jean-Jacques' critics" (Boucher 1992: 118, 123).

Endogenous and exogenous inferiorization reflects modernity's fixations. As modernity fixes its attention on a process immanent in the human condition, in other words, the activity of improving, of enhancing, of making better, it fetishizes newness and the "modern" is codified as progress, whereas lack of it is devolved to the premodern, nonmodern, or antimodern, which are now deemed static or regressive. This is "the irrational myth of modernity" that Dussel speaks of, or what Zygmunt Bauman and Amy Allen have called "the self-confidence of the present" and "self-congratulation," respectively (Allen 2017: 31; Bauman 2000: 132; Dussel 1996: 52).

"A degenerate people," in Edward Gibbon's view, the Byzantines "held in their lifeless hands the riches of their fathers, without inheriting the spirit which had created and improved that sacred patrimony: they read, they praised, they compiled, but their languid souls seemed alike incapable of thought and action." For Gibbon, "in the revolution of ten centuries, not a single discovery was made to exalt the dignity or promote the happiness of mankind. Not a single idea has been added to the speculative systems of antiquity." The eighteenth-century historian insists that "not a single composition of history, philosophy, or literature, has been saved from oblivion by the intrinsic beauties of style or sentiment, of original fancy, or even of successful imitation." But despite catapulting Byzantium to the abyss of darkness, Gibbon's conclusion is that "by the assiduous study of the ancients," the Byzantines deserve, "in some measure, the remembrance and gratitude of the moderns." About a century later, the French historian Jules Zeller would call the Byzantines "the librarians of humanity" ("les bibliothécaires du genre humain") (Gibbon 1997: 514–516; Zeller 1871: 393).

In the history of western thought, Byzantium plays the unenviable role of preserving and occasionally of renovating, but never truly of innovating the

Greco-Roman past. Gibbon's negative depiction of Byzantium, writes Fiona Haarer citing the English historian, led to the problematic but dominant view of it "as a product of 'the triumph of barbarism and Christianity'." Prejudiced by the values and moral biases of the Enlightenment and the Italian Renaissance, Gibbon hastily dismissed Byzantium's accomplishments across different spheres. It was his "sentiments," says Haarer, together with the Eurocentrism of Victorian society and its moralizing environment which later influenced historians like William Lecky, who declared that "of that Byzantine empire, the universal verdict of history is that it constitutes without a single exception, the most thoroughly base and despicable form that civilization has yet assumed." Byzantium, Lecky concluded, was "absolutely destitute of all the forms and elements of greatness" (Haarer 2010: 11–12; Lecky 1869: 13).[7] Among the Enlightenment thinkers that Haarer mentions are Montesquieu, who in his *Considerations on the Causes of the Greatness of the Romans and Their Decline* (1734) understood the history of Byzantium as "a tissue of revolts, seditions and perfidies," Voltaire, who described it as a "worthless collection [which] contains nothing but declamations and miracles," calling it "a disgrace to the human mind," and Hegel, whose indictment of Byzantium is unparalleled. In his *Lectures on the Philosophy of History*, published posthumously in 1837, the German philosopher argues that "the realm was in a condition of perpetual insecurity. Its general aspect presents a disgusting picture of imbecility; wretched, nay, insane passions, stifle the growth of all that is noble in thoughts, deeds, and persons." The "rotten" foundations of the Eastern Roman Empire, he writes, whose history is steeped in rebellions, intrigues, assassinations, and all sorts of abominations, in the end "crumbled in pieces before the might of the vigorous Turks" (in Haarer 2010: 10–12; Hegel 2004: 340). According to him, Byzantium exhibits "a most repulsive and consequently a most uninteresting picture" (Hegel 2004: 338).

In this way, a disparaging discourse about Byzantium emerges during the Enlightenment, one that fed into modernity's rhetoric of superiority, whose continuing impact may be seen in contemporary negative usages of the epithet "Byzantine". The dictionaries of the French and Royal Spanish Academies and various Italian lexica report the adjectives *byzantin* and *bizantino* in relation to an argument or discussion that is "affected," "contrived," "excessively subtle," "futile," "pedantic," "captious," and "decadent."[8] In German, *byzantinisch* stands

---

[7] For western European scholarship on Byzantium from the seventeenth to the nineteenth centuries, see Vasiliev (1952: 3–31).

[8] "Dicho de una discusión: Artificiosa o demasiado sutil" (*Diccionario de la lengua española de la Real Academia Española*); "*Querelle, discussion byzantine*, d'une subtilité excessive et sans intérêt réel, par allusion aux controverses grammaticales ou théologiques des derniers temps de

for "fawning," "unctuous," "obsequious," "groveling," and "sycophantic," while the Oxford Dictionary of English tells us that we can use *byzantine* to refer to "a system or situation" that is "excessively complicated, typically involving a great deal of administrative detail," providing as an example the expression "Byzantine insurance regulations."[9] A second meaning of the epithet as that which is "characterized by deviousness or underhand procedure" is illustrated with the phrase "he has the most Byzantine mind in politics."[10]

Since the Enlightenment, Byzantium has been relegated to the backstage of epistemic history, sometimes even in academic fields that actively question modernity's coloniality, such as ecocritical, postcolonial, and decolonial studies. In Cheryll Glotfelty and Harold Fromm's influential *The Ecocriticism Reader* we find reprinted a 1967 article by the medievalist historian Lynn White who reiterates the idea of Byzantium as static and anti-innovative, arguing that the Byzantines seem "to have produced no marked technological innovation after the late seventh century, when Greek fire was invented." He goes on to claim that "always in the Greek East, nature was conceived primarily as a symbolic system through which God speaks to men: the ant is a sermon to sluggards; rising flames are the symbol of the soul's aspiration. This view of nature was essentially artistic rather than scientific." His conclusion is well known: "While Byzantium preserved and copied great numbers of ancient Greek scientific texts, science as we conceive it could scarcely flourish in such an ambience" (White 1996: 10–11).[11] Adam Goldwyn rightly points out in his pioneering work *Byzantine Ecocriticism* that "these kinds of inaccurate generalizations will continue to warp non-Byzantinists' understanding of the

---

l'empire de Byzance" (*Dictionnaire de l'Académie Française*). Also, "qui évoque, par son excès de subtilité, par son caractère formel et oiseux, les disputes théologiques de Byzance" (*Le Petit Robert*), and "discussions subtiles et oiseuses, sans objet ni intérêt réels" (*Grand Larousse de la langue française*). The Italian use of the term *bizantino* is still negative, although slightly milder: "eccessivamente raffinato, decadente," "esageratamente minuzioso, pedante" (*Grande dizionario italiano dell'uso*) and "cavilloso, pedantesco" (*Dizionario della lingua italiana*). *Dizionario della lingua italiana* also reports "prezioso" (intricate) and "raffinato" (refined, subtle) – without the adverb "eccessivamente" – along with "decadente."

[9] "Schmeichlerisch, unterwürfig" (*Wahrig deutsches Wörterbuch*) and "kriecherisch" (*Duden: das große Wörterbuch der deutschen Sprache*).

[10] In *Byzantine Matters* (2014), Averil Cameron addresses the general absence of Byzantium from western historiography, arguing that "part of the reason for Byzantium's absence from the wider historical discourse is that it has been relegated to the sphere of negativity" (Cameron 2014: 10).

[11] In the same article, White famously attributed the roots of the ecological crisis to "the Christian axiom that nature has no reason for existence save to serve man" (White 1996: 14). Among the many critics of this idea is Joshtrom Isaac Kureethadam, who argues that "the triple foundations of the Modern worldview – in terms of an exaggerated anthropocentrism, a mechanistic conception of the natural world, and the metaphysical dualism between humanity and the rest of the physical world – can all be largely traced back to the Cartesian thought with direct ecological consequences" (Kureethadam 2017: 5). See also note 38 in this Element.

period." He adds that "perhaps more damning than inaccurate overgeneraliza-
tions [. . .] is the widespread silence about Byzantium that pervades ecocritical
discourse and other contemporary theoretical fields." We should remember, he
says, that "much yet remains unknown about the environmental attitudes of
a multifaceted culture that lasted a thousand years and covered large and
ecologically diverse swathes of three continents and the seas and waterways
that linked them" (Goldwyn 2018: 21).

Similarly, despite his perceptive critique of western constructions of the East as
"static," "frozen," and lacking "development," "transformation," and "human
movement," Said does not avoid an orientalist view of Byzantium as motionless
and inert, able only to preserve in its "lifeless hands," according to Gibbon, the
knowledge of antiquity. Because the Renaissance humanists appropriated the
knowledge of "dead people," Said reasons, such appropriation was trouble-free
as opposed to "modern times" when "cultural exchange" necessarily involves
"domination and forcible appropriation: someone loses, someone gains." "The
Greek classics," he writes, "served the Italian, French, and English humanists
without the troublesome interposition of actual Greeks. Texts by dead people
were read, appreciated, and appropriated by people who imagined an ideal
commonwealth. This is one reason that scholars rarely speak suspiciously or
disparagingly of the Renaissance" (Said 1979: 208; Said 1994: 195). Said
overlooks the fact that the west's Byzantine borrowings involved at least as
much domination and forcible appropriation, particularly during the Fourth
Crusade (1202–1204) which ended with the Latin sack of Constantinople, as
cultural exchange in modern times does. And although the interaction between
Byzantium, Islam, and the west during the Middle Ages was beneficial to all, the
one who profited most, in Deno Geanakoplos's terms, was "the backward Latin
west" (Geanakoplos 1993: 208). At least until the Crusader sack of the empire's
capital city in 1204, the Byzantines considered themselves "the exclusive heirs to
the superior Roman political and Hellenic cultural heritage" and therefore the
carriers of civilization. And because of this, they consistently viewed the Latin
west as "barbarians" or "semi-barbarians" (Stouraitis 2022: 21–22).

Commenting on Said's passage, Robert Nelson notes the author's failure to
realize that the Greek literature of the Italian Renaissance "was appropriated
from people, who were very much alive. They referred to themselves as Romans
and later as Hellenes. It is we who call them Byzantines and assign to the epithet
'Byzantine' connotations that are very much a part of orientalism." Said's
statement echoes the well-known argument, which was formulated in the
nineteenth century and is still current today, that "because easterners could
not properly appreciate what they had, westerners were the proper custodians of
their artifacts" (Nelson 1995: 234–235). Focusing on the relationship between

Byzantinism and orientalism, Przemysław Marciniak argues that the field of Byzantine studies developed, after a long pause, in the nineteenth century alongside the flourishing of orientalist studies and that several scholars shared both interests. Many nineteenth-century works, he mentions, draw on orientalist imagery to describe Byzantium (Marciniak 2018: 49–50). It is not surprising, then, that Byzantium was finally orientalized.

Panagiotis Agapitos says that the orientalist attitude toward Byzantium, which had progressively developed in the west from the seventeenth century and was strengthened by nineteenth-century colonialism, solidified European notions of the West as culturally superior. Viewed through the orientalist lens as exotic, luxurious, sensual, mysterious, despotic, and languid, the East emerged as the inferior opposite to "the frugal, familiar, luminous, intellectual, vigorous, democratic West." Gibbon's presentation of Byzantium as an entity in millennial decline led to its portrayal as a "monolithic administrative system." In this way, eighteenth-century scholars had a perfect example of an oriental empire and Byzantium ultimately turned into "a medieval version of the Ottoman Empire." As the offspring of orientalism and nationalism, Agapitos concludes, this viewpoint enabled westerners to locate the beginnings of European states in the medieval west, even if the medieval period had been repudiated at some point, and also allowed them to claim the legacy of Greek antiquity through the Roman Empire and the Italian Renaissance, despite the fact that direct knowledge of Greek culture and language arrived to the west via the Byzantines. Meanwhile, according to Gibbon's historical paradigm, "Byzantium was not included among the national medieval states" and was therefore "expelled from Europe's historical progress" (Agapitos 1992: 237–238).[12]

On this point, Yannis Stouraitis writes that the expulsion of the Eastern Roman Empire from the west's symbolic territory and its historical canon was enabled by the renaming of the medieval Roman Empire of Constantinople as Byzantium. Unlike the term "Roman" (in Greek "Romaios"), the word "Byzantine" denoting the empire and its subjects existed, like Said's "Orient," only within modern historiography. In this way, Stouraitis argues, it was much easier to attribute the notion of an oriental kingdom to Byzantium and think of it as the antecedent of an oriental empire like the Ottoman Empire as opposed to the medieval descendant and heir of ancient Rome. The terms "Byzantium" and "Byzantines" were coined to sustain an essentialized and idealized image of Greek and Roman classical antiquity, free of any medieval transmutations. Byzantinism, as a historiographical discourse introduced by Gibbon, was extrinsic to the Eastern Roman society (Stouraitis 2022: 21–23, 25, 27).[13]

---

[12] On Byzantium and orientalism, see also Cameron (2003).

[13] On the term "Byzantinism," see Angelov (2003), Stamatopoulos (2013), and Bodin (2016).

Anthony Kaldellis explains that the intellectuals of the Enlightenment put forward the image of Byzantium as a specific type of theocracy, projecting it as an anti-model to indirectly examine contemporary issues. Those thinkers, he says, were not really concerned with the actual Byzantium. For them, it was a handy model which they used in line with their own political agendas, treating it as a "mirror" to reflect the facets of their contemporary societies that they sought to eradicate. Byzantium "has played the role of 'the absolutist Orthodox Christian empire' in the western imagination for so long that it is hard to think of it as anything else. No small dose of Orientalism has been poured into this recipe" (Kaldellis 2015: 8, 97, 200). Kaldellis is no doubt right about Byzantium's distorted reflection in the funhouse mirror of the Enlightenment and the social and political purposes that lurk behind it. But it is important to remember that this partisan image was ultimately forged dialectically in response to modernity's self-imagining, in other words, it arose from the Enlightenment fixation with rationalism, or *logolatry*. In the modern consciousness, Byzantium's alleged theocracy or *theolatry* came to stand for what the Enlightenment supposedly did not. "The theocratic ideology abides," asserts Kaldellis, despite a determined effort in recent years to oppose many features of that "polemical model," adding that it is difficult to appreciate why this is the case (Kaldellis 2015: 8).

The polemical model, in my opinion, persists because it is part of the foundational narrative of the Enlightenment and as such is inextricably related to the rhetorical construction of the "modern." The orientalist view of the Byzantine Empire is emblematic of modernity's coloniality at home. The imagery of Byzantium as static and epistemically moribund, when in fact it played a key and active role in setting the stage for European modernity either directly or via Islam, is one of the irrational myths of modernity. That this imagery retains currency today reveals that despite our diligent efforts in decolonial and postcolonial studies, the colonial gaze of the Enlightenment continues to loom large in our critical discussions and, even more so, in our collective consciousness. The Byzantine Empire, of course, was not fossilized, but our vision of it is.

In *The Underside of Modernity* (1996), Dussel argues that modernity is originally a European phenomenon whose sources can be found in the Babylonian, Egyptian, Greek, and Semitic worlds. The colonization of the Americas, he says, allowed Europe (what he calls "a particular 'ecumene' without evident comparative advantages up to then") to "overcome all other ecumenes" of the time (Dussel 1996: 132). Likewise, in *The Invention of the Americas* (1995) he notes that until 1492, western Europe was peripheral to the Islamic world. "Hemmed in by the Turks at Vienna on the east until 1681," western Europe "had never been the center of history," he observes, adding that from Seville to Vienna, the Latin-Germanic west was never more than a hundred million people and was therefore demographically smaller than China. Dussel sees the birth of modernity coinciding with the end of Europe's long confinement. Thanks to the Portuguese, it arrives in India, Japan, and Africa; thanks to the Spaniards, it reaches Latin America and the Philippines. This is the moment when Europe becomes center (Dussel 1995: 88, 90; Dussel 1996: 52).[14]

Considering the west's peripheral standing prior to modernity, Dussel accuses Hegel of succumbing to "myopic Eurocentrism" when he refers to Europe "as the beginning, center, and end of world history" (Dussel 1995: 90). Kant's theory of immaturity, whose seeds Dussel traces in the Spanish theologian Ginés de Sepúlveda's treatise *Concerning the Just Cause of the War Against the Indians* (1547), particularly in his Aristotelian notion of the indigenous peoples as natural slaves, will be later employed by Hegel in a "global historical vision." Hegel's famous Eurocentric assumption, Dussel writes quoting the German philosopher, is that world history flows from east to west because "Europe is the absolute end of history." Western Europe, "which includes Germany, France, Denmark, and Scandinavia, is *the heart of Europe*." According to Dussel, Hegel's view of southern Europe is limited to the Italian Renaissance, whereas Spain remains "outside history" (Dussel 1996: 51–52, 60, original emphasis). Dussel's critique of "the irrational myth of modernity" is not without flaws, though. When it comes to Byzantium, one of Islam's and western Europe's primary interlocutors, his revisionist Islamocentric view appears to be at least partially myopic.

Dussel seems to dismiss the factor Byzantium. Appendix I of *The Invention of the Americas* provides a series of encyclopedia-like entries on the "diverse meanings of the terms Europe, the Occident, Modernity, Late Capitalism" spanning from classical Greece to the twentieth century. Here Constantinople and the Byzantine Empire are variously called "Christian Roman Empire" (seventh century), "Orient," "Greek Orthodoxy" (twelfth century), and "Greek Orient" (fifteenth century) (Dussel 1995: 133–134). None of these schematic references address Byzantium's impact on the Italian Renaissance, but instead indicate a lack of engagement and unease in historicizing Byzantium's role in laying the groundwork for western modernity.[15] In his later work, Dussel seems to partially rectify this oversight. Specifically, in *The Underside of Modernity* there is a brief comment in a footnote, according to which "Byzantism" belongs as much to the Latin west as to

---

[14] Dussel would later add that "this period of the European 'first modernity' [...] only developed with hegemony over the Atlantic [...]. European modernity was still peripheral to the Hindustani and Chinese world, and even to the Islamic one in terms of links to the 'East'" (Dussel 2002: 228).

[15] In *The Invention of the Americas* there are two further references to Byzantium as a "version" of Christianity, which add little to the discussion (Dussel 1995: 54, 111).

Islam, without any mention of Byzantium itself: "Modern Western culture has attempted and achieved a 'kidnapping' of classical Greek culture as an exclusive European moment. There is no clear consciousness of the fact that classical Greece, and even the Byzantism, is as much Arab-Muslim as it is Latin-Christian" (Dussel 1996: 149). We come across a similar statement in his article "Europe, Modernity, and Eurocentrism" (2000), where he notes that from the seventh century on classical Greek antiquity was "as much Arab Muslim as Byzantine Christian" and that "the resurgence of Platonic thought in fifteenth-century Italy was of Christian Byzantine origin." Here Dussel acknowledges Byzantium's contribution to the Renaissance via the transmission of ancient Greek knowledge in the fourteenth and fifteenth centuries. His formulaic approach, however, visualized in a flow chart with the title "Historical sequence from the Greek to the modern European world," makes the puzzling observation that "there is no direct Greek influence on western Latin Europe" prior to the fourteenth century, and that from the tenth century on such influence was the exclusive enterprise of the Arab Muslim and Jewish worlds acting as an intermediary between Greek antiquity and western Europe (Dussel 2000: 466–467, 476). Equally baffling is the absence in Dussel's flow chart of a direct contact between the Byzantine Empire and Islam when, in fact, until the late thirteenth century "politically, economically, and culturally, the Arab authors still hold Constantinople in the highest regard" (El-Cheikh 2001: 63).[16] It is suggested that Byzantium's lack of consequence can be seen not just in its inability to generate new knowledge, but also in its failure to directly communicate its heritage.

Dussel's argument is clearly flawed, not least because it ignores key historical facts, including the cultural exchanges between Byzantium and Islam which were heightened in the ninth and tenth centuries, a period which Geanakoplos considers the most fertile in terms of transmission of knowledge from the Byzantines to the Arabs since the conquest of the eastern provinces in the seventh century (Geanakoplos 1993: 202), the flight of Byzantine monks and manuscripts to Italy during the Iconoclastic period (eighth and ninth centuries), Byzantium's dominance over southern Italy until the Norman conquest in 1071, and, crucially, the Crusader sacking of Constantinople in 1204, which resulted in the direct migration of Greek knowledge to the medieval west. To these, we should add the numerous documented diplomatic and mercantile contacts

---

[16] Referring to the middle Byzantine period (843–1204), Priscilla Soucek notes that "despite the strong antagonism that existed between the Byzantine emperors and their Islamic rivals, a shared culture of court ceremonial and a common enthusiasm for luxury goods aided their communication. Other artistic and cultural ties were also forged between the two societies. A mutual interest in the scientific legacy of antiquity created bonds between scholars on both sides" (Soucek 1997: 411).

between the Latin west and Byzantium, which served as a springboard for the exchange of cultural capital throughout the Middle Ages.[17] Alexander Kazhdan makes reference to the Byzantine warriors who "entered the lists and crossed arms with western knights," the marriages of members of the Byzantine nobility with westerners, the "Latin blood" that flowed through the veins of Byzantium's royal dynasties, the numerous Byzantine theologians who found common ground in dialogue with Western peers, and the Italian merchants who established themselves in various Byzantine trading posts (Kazhdan 1995: 4).

Referring to Byzantine artifacts that we know were in the Latin west from about 850 to 1261, William Wixom explains that a raft of them ended up in the west as diplomatic gifts, while others were commissioned or bought in Constantinople, and yet more were obtained by visitors in transit cities like Pavia and Rome. He goes on to add that in the early ninth century, Pope Pascal I (r. 817–24) and before him Pope Leo III (r. 795–816) offered to churches in Ravenna and Rome silks that may have been produced by Byzantines trying to flee Iconoclasm, and that with the Latin sack of Constantinople in the early thirteenth century, many more objects found their way to western Europe as loot. Wixom points out that this transfer of cultural goods unfolded against a backdrop of people on the move, among them kings and princes, imperial diplomatic envoys, artists, scholars, traders, and clergymen, as well as the looting armies of the Crusaders who traveled between western Europe, the Holy Land, and Byzantium. The latter, he says, "was increasingly regarded in the West with a mixture of awe, amazement, respect, competitiveness, envy, and covetousness" (Wixom 1997: 435, 442).[18] Nelson offers a concrete example of a direct influence in his reference to the fifth-century Byzantine illuminated manuscript Cotton Genesis, which was used as the model for San Marco's atrium mosaics in Venice, dating from the 1220s (Nelson 1995: 213–214).

Dussel's view of Byzantium is anything but novel. The Eastern Roman Empire, by no means culturally peripheral to Islam at least up until 1204, has

---

[17] Geanakoplos, for example, mentions the brief visit of the "pro-Western" Byzantine scholar Maximos Planoudes as an ambassador of the Byzantine emperor in Venice in 1296, adding that "he had translated into Greek various Latin writings of Ovid, Macrobius, Augustine, and Boethius" (Geanakoplos 1962: 27). Fausto Montana notes that Planoudes translated several Greek works into Latin, including Ptolemy's *Geography*, "which were among the first to circulate in the west" (Montana 2011: 38).

[18] Nadia Maria El-Cheikh informs us that "the Arab authors of the twelfth and thirteenth centuries reiterated the now entrenched belief of the Byzantines' unequaled skill in building, craftsmanship, and painting" and that "unlike the Western view of Constantinople, which moves from praise to denigration, the Arabic texts of the twelfth and thirteenth centuries rarely, if ever, include negative comments." She observes that in the Arabic texts of the time, the Crusaders are "deemed unworthy inferiors in comparison with the sophisticated and refined Byzantines," adding that "during this period, the Byzantines alongside the Muslims became the target of the Crusaders' offensive" (El-Cheikh 2001: 55–57, 62, 68).

long been treated as an epistemic backwater hobbled by dogma and despotism. Its marginalization, in Maria Mavroudi's words, is the result of a narrative that was formulated in the context of European colonialism, according to which the cultural heritage of Greco-Roman antiquity, presumably coming to an end in the sixth century, is transmitted to Islam from the seventh century onward. The Muslim world preserves and enhances the philosophy and science of the ancients until the twelfth century when, thanks to a fresh wave of Latin translations from Arabic, these are "transplanted into the 'west', where they are subsequently elaborated, contributing to its economic and political supremacy." In line with this narrative, Mavroudi adds, the Byzantines in the meantime preserved the knowledge of the Greco-Roman world until they passed it on to western Europe via its scholars who were leaving the empire around the time of the Ottoman conquest of Constantinople in 1453, taking with them precious manuscripts (Mavroudi 2013: 6063–6064; Mavroudi 2024: 175–176).[19]

I have argued that with the Greco-Roman and Islamic contributions to modernity duly acknowledged and the image of the western Middle Ages gradually rehabilitated, the formulaic trope of the abyss of darkness and the idea of a theocratic hiatus on the grand scale of universal progress have been retained for the Eastern Roman Empire, widely regarded as unoriginal, progress-phobic, regressive, or inert. The fact that a lot of Byzantine scientific texts continue to remain unpublished to date is indicative of the long-held perception of Byzantium as a fossilized culture, "introverted, unable to receive anything from the outside, preoccupied by rehashing its own ancient heritage" (Mavroudi 2013: 6063). Plinio Prioreschi, who traced the idea of scientific progress in Greco-Roman antiquity, the Islamic world, and the western Middle Ages dismisses Byzantium. Referring to medicine in particular, he passes on the old chestnut that the Byzantines frequently saw medicine as perfected or completed (*ars perfecta*), with no room left for improvement (Prioreschi 2002: 37). Prioreschi's disregard for Byzantine medicine is symptomatic of the general view of Byzantium as unimaginative and incapable of epistemic advancement. And yet recent research in Byzantine science, especially in the history of medicine, forces us to reconsider this position.[20] In many ways, writes Mavroudi, Byzantine science was "no 'better' or 'worse' than its ancient Greek and medieval Arabic equivalents. [...] [T]he modern understanding of science as an intellectual good that is passed over as a torch from one civilisation to the next (from the ancient Near East to Graeco-Roman antiquity to the medieval Islamicate world and early modern Europe) needs to be revisited" (Mavroudi 2024: 176). Aside from medicine, the

---

[19] See also Mavroudi (2015).
[20] See, for instance, Lazaris (2020a) and Bouras-Vallianatos (2020).

Byzantines displayed tangible innovations in the spheres of health care, astronomy, mathematics, architecture, chemistry, technology, physics, geography, art, and education, particularly during Byzantium's three renaissances – the Macedonian (mid ninth to tenth centuries), the Komnenian (twelfth century), and the Palaiologan (mid thirteenth to mid fifteenth centuries) – which make Eltjo Buringh speak of a "more or less permanent 'renaissance'" (Buringh 2011: 142).[21] A long-overdue revisionary reading of Byzantium is now gathering momentum, but it will need to reach audiences beyond Byzantine Studies.

The negative view of Byzantium outside and occasionally within the circles of Byzantinists is clear evidence of modernity's enduring coloniality, as is, we shall see, the current ecological crisis. The Moderns thought of Byzantium and nature as inert entities and as reservoirs of epistemic and material wealth. The Byzantines were the librarians of humanity, while nature was a bottomless pit of natural resources, both valuable to the emergence and consolidation of the modern. When seen in this light, it is evident that the colonial image of Byzantium and the ecological crisis are intrinsically intertwined. Almost three centuries after the Crusader sack of Constantinople and thirty-nine years after its Ottoman conquest, coloniality as the constitutive element of modernity is about to fully unfold overseas. In Giovanni Stradano's (Jan van der Straet) print *Christopher Columbus on his Ship* (Figure 1) from the series *Discovery of America* dating from the late 1580s, the Genoese admiral appears as the "heroic crusader" on the cusp of modernity, which he inaugurates with a banner bearing the crucified Christ in one hand and a nautical map in the other (Markey 2012: 412). This is modernity in the making. The discursive constructions of the indigenous peoples as savages or infantile and of Byzantium as static or retrograde are tributaries of the same river – the river of modernity. Byzantium and America inevitably became unlikely partners in modernity.

---

[21] For a discussion of Byzantine science vis-à-vis modern science, see Lazaris (2020b: 21–22) and Pérez Martín and Manolova (2020: 53–59). Kazhdan observes that "there was both imitation and innovation in Byzantium, and, surprisingly or not, the more the Byzantines imitated (or studied) antiquity the more innovative they became," while Robert Browning speaks of "an ever-changing and dialectical relation between past and present in the world of the Byzantines" (Browning 1995: 28; Kazdhan 1995: 11). For a survey of the current state of knowledge about Byzantine medicine and pharmacy, see Touwaide (2020). For more on Byzantine epistemic innovations and achievements in medicine, health care, astronomy, mathematics, architecture, technology, physics, geography, art, and education, see: Agapitos (2003, 2015), Anastos (1952, 1962), Bennett (2016), Bouras-Vallianatos (2020), Chroni (2010), El-Cheikh (2001), Fry (1996), Geanakoplos (1984), Guilland (1926), Haas (1996), Horden (2005), Kazhdan (1991), Kolias (2005), Langslow (2013), Lazaris (2020c), Lemerle (1986), Littlewood (1995), Magdalino (2013), Markopoulos (2008), Mavroudi (2013, 2024), Mayor (2013), McCabe (2007), McGeer (1991), Miller (1997), Mitrović (2004), Mylonas et al. (2015), Nelson (2004a, 2004b, 2015), Oberhelman (2013), Ousterhout (2015), Papadakis et al. (2014, 2015), Pentogalos and Lascaratos (1984), Poulakou-Rebelakou (2000), Poulakou-Rebelakou et al. (2011), Salmon (2020), Scarborough (1997), Scarborough and Cutler (1991), Taroutina (2015), Temkin (1962), Tihon (2013), Traka (2007), Treadgold (1984), Verpeaux (1959), and Zagklas (2017, 2018).

CHRISTOPHORVS COLVMBVS LIGVR. *terroribus Oceani, superatis alterius pene Orbis regiones à se inventas Hispanis regibus addixit. An.salutis ꝏ.VIIID.*

Figure 1 "Christopher Columbus on his Ship," from *The Discovery of America* (*Americae Retectio*) series, Adriaen Collaert, after Jan van der Straet, engraving, c. 1589. © The Trustees of the British Museum.

We know that the Moderns saw America as a blank slate onto which their epistemic system could be written; it was viewed as a testing ground for European modernity. The exogenous histories of its peoples would be inferiorized first on religious grounds by conquistadors and missionaries, and then on scientific grounds by the intellectuals of the Enlightenment. The Franciscan missionary Diego de Landa mentions the burning of Maya books in sixteenth-century Mexico in his book *On the Things of Yucatan*, written about 1566. "We found a large number of books," he reports, "and, as they contained nothing in which there was not to be seen superstition and lies of the devil, we burned them all, which they regretted to an amazing degree and which caused them great affliction" (in Clendinnen 2003: 70). The indigenous are seen as bereft of religion, superstitious, and unrefined, their histories as premodern, and their epistemic systems as regressive or belated in comparison to western Europe. This resulted in indigenous epistemicide, or the systematic elimination of local knowledge, as well as in the irrational myth of modernity abroad. The colonized were believed to be lacking in civilization, which should be brought to them through European intervention, whether via Christianization, or modernization, or both. With their three major civilizations, the Mexica, Inca, and Maya, reportedly dead, the premodern or nonmodern peoples of America were challenged to catch up with European modernity and its alleged epistemic superiority throughout the colonial period.

Preconquest America, like Byzantium, demonstrates epistemic accomplishments across all spheres of life. If our understanding of Byzantium is limited because of the loss of countless manuscripts during the two sackings of Constantinople, our knowledge of indigenous cultures is further curtailed due to the destruction of written material. However, surviving evidence tells us that pre-Columbian Americans displayed great achievements in engineering, architecture, physics, and mechanics, as proven by their bridges and high roadways, their urban organization, their sophisticated agricultural techniques, and their coastal navigation that commercially connected peoples living in different areas (D'Ambrosio 1977: 274). America's most sophisticated precontact cultures also showed significant accomplishments in medicine, surgery, pharmacology, mathematics, astronomy, chemistry, education, and artistry, among others.[22]

Needless to say, the epistemic achievements of pre-Columbian America, Byzantium, and other premodern civilizations are not meant to be compared or contrasted with those of modernity as such comparisons would be naïve and pointless. But keeping in mind those accomplishments could alert us to the fallacy inherent in modernity's rhetoric of exceptionalism, especially when modern epistemic conquests are put in historical perspective. Stradano's frontispiece for the *New Discoveries* series (*Nova Reperta*) (1580s) (Figure 2) contains an early visualization of modernity's narrative of exceptionalism.[23] The "new discoveries" are announced in a cartouche at the upper center of the engraving, while the distance between modernity and antiquity is illustrated in the allegory of two figures, the first, young and vigorous on the left entering the frame and the second, aged with a beard and a hunched back exiting to the right. With a staff in the right hand, the youthful figure of this epic visual narrative points to the map of America within the roundel on the left, which reads: "Christophor. Columbus Genuens. inventor" (Gombrich 1998: 195–196; Smith 2006: 90). Columbus embodies the prodigious European, the modern man as inventor, even if most of the "new" inventions depicted here are neither modern nor western in origin. America, the magnetic compass, gunpowder

---

[22] For more information, see Aguilar-Moreno (2007), Bastien (1982), Berdan (2014), Bray (1985), Candiani (2014), Carlson (1975), Clendinnen (1991), Closs (1996), D'Altroy (2003), D'Ambrosio (1977), Finger (1994), Foster (2005), Hardoy (1973), Kaplan (2000), León-Portilla (1963), López Austin and López Luján (2001), Malmström (2008), Malpass (2009), Mendoza (1997, 2003), Mundy (2015), Ortiz de Montellano (1990), Pennock (2013), Sutton and Anderson (2014), Tannenbaum (2012), Verano (2016), and Viesca (2003).

[23] The *Nova Reperta* series comprises nineteen prints, "each representing a different invention or discovery of the recent centuries" (Markey 2012: 386).

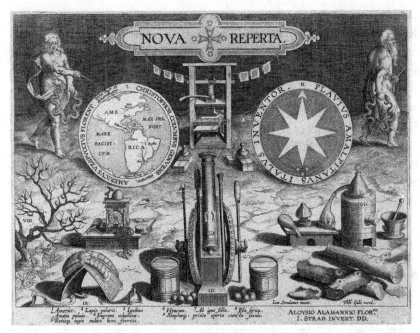

Figure 2 Frontispiece for the *New Discoveries* (*Nova Reperta*) series, Jan Collaert (II) (attributed to), after Jan van der Straet, engraving, c. 1589. Rijksmuseum, Amsterdam, CC0, courtesy of Wikimedia Commons.

weapons, the printing press, the mechanical clock, *guaiacum* wood, distillation, silk, and stirrups are all mentioned in the caption of Stradano's print. Six of these "discoveries" have been famously traced back to China by Joseph Needham. The compass, gunpowder, the printing press, the mechanical clock, silk, and stirrups, he says, were directly inherited from China, "at the very least by stimulus diffusion."[24] He goes on to say that as the inventors of the compass and the sternpost rudder, the Chinese also contributed to the discovery of America and Europe's access to indigenous medicinal plants like the *guaiacum*, which was thought to be a remedy for syphilis (Gombrich 1998: 196; Needham 2000: 6–8).

Distillation, adds Needham, was common to Chinese and Greek antiquity and most probably spread rapidly among nomadic peoples in Asia, an idea shared by Ernst Gombrich, who argues that an Arabic influence in the case of distillation is

---

[24] With respect to the mechanical clock, Ernst Gombrich notes that although "the Greco-Roman world was far advanced in the construction of mechanical gears, [...] they lacked the vital contribution of the escapement that secures even movement," adding that Needham "established beyond reasonable doubt that the Chinese had priority over the West in the construction of such a device, but it is possible that an analogous mechanism was developed independently in the West in the thirteenth century" (Gombrich 1998: 197–198).

at least likely. The invention of the magnetic compass depicted in the roundel on the right is wrongly attributed to Flavio Gioia (Flavius Amalfitanus Inventor) and *guaiacum* was a "false hope," notes Gombrich, because it did not cure syphilis. We do not know to what extent Stradano was familiar with the origins of the inventions he depicted, Gombrich concludes, but the fact that he considers the magnetic compass an invention of Flavio Gioia suggests the contrary (Gombrich 1998: 196, 198–199; Needham 2000: 8).

Even though the new discoveries or modern inventions (the noun *inventio* accepts both meanings) are neither entirely new nor completely modern, in Stradano's late sixteenth-century prints we see embedded the logic of a reflexive modernity about to reinvent itself as both exceptional and exceptionally innovative. This process would culminate with the Enlightenment and nineteenth-century positivist thinking. "We can now scarcely conceive of such a state of things," Auguste Comte claimed, referring to the "primitive" or "theological" stage of thinking, "our reason having become sufficiently mature to enter upon laborious scientific researches, without needing any such stimulus as wrought upon the imaginations of astrologers and alchemists" (Comte 1858: 27–28). But beneath Comte's words, we can read that without those astrologers and alchemists, without the compass, the printing press, and the gunpowder – a fortuitous innovation of Chinese alchemists (Glick 2013: 34) – without the innumerable epistemic attainments of Byzantium, Islam, China, America, and so many other ancient civilizations, modern science would most certainly be confined to the realm of western imagination.

We know that a great part of modernity's achievements did not originate exclusively in Europe but resulted from a constant "dialectic of impact and counter-impact [...] between modern Europe and its periphery" (Dussel 1996: 132). America's material and epistemic contributions to the expansion of modernity worldwide were critical and incalculable. The silver mine of Potosí in present-day Bolivia is just one among countless examples of America's material contribution to the rise of the modern. Discovered in 1545 in the territory of the former Inca Empire, Potosí, writes Thomas Cummins, "transformed the global notion of wealth and value. It was the envy of all other European states and enabled a new global market." In the sixteenth century, Potosí's Cerro Rico, or Rich Mountain, fueled trade internationally by providing three-fifths of the world's silver supply. The expression *vale un Perú* (worth a Peru), or *vale un Potosí* (worth a Potosí), "recognizes the discovery in 1545 of the richest silver mine ever encountered" (Cummins 2012: 407, 411).

Without Potosí, says Neil MacGregor, the history of Europe in the sixteenth century would not have been the same. American silver allowed the Spanish kings to become the most powerful leaders in Europe, financing their armadas and armies. But even though the raw material produced by the mine of Potosí made Spain wealthy, it was the Potosí mint that was responsible for laying the groundwork for a global currency by producing the *peso de ocho reales*, or "silver pieces of eight," which MacGregor calls "the first truly global money." He explains that the coins were carried by llamas to the Pacific coast and Lima through the Andes. From there, the bullion was taken by Spanish vessels to Panama, where it was transported by land across the isthmus and subsequently in convoys across the Atlantic. Spain's Asian empire, which was based in the Philippines, meant that the silver trade was not restricted to Europe. Pieces of eight were traded in Manila, typically with merchants from China, for porcelain, but also for ivory, spices, silks, and lacquer. The *peso de ocho reales* produced financial instability in Ming China and destabilized the economies of East Asia. In fact, there was barely "any part of the world that remained unaffected by these ubiquitous coins" (MacGregor 2011: 517–520).

Potosí impacted world economy since the sixteenth century, "contributing directly to the Industrial Revolution." The inclusion of the mine, referred to as "Pei-tu-shi," in a sixteenth-century map from China reflects Potosí's importance in international trade and its contribution to the rise of global economy (Cruz 2006: 36). Cummins rightly points out in his discussion of Martín de Murúa's allegorical image of the mine (Figure 3) dating from the late sixteenth century (Codex Galvin) that the composition recalls the connection between Peru and Spain, the colonial present and the Inca past. The Rich Mountain, he writes, is depicted schematically while the figures' scale does not match the size of the mountain because the artist did not seek a realistic representation. The gigantic Inca figure who "dwarfs the great mountain, embracing the two columns that represent the Pillars of Hercules" allegorically supports the empire as he pronounces "I hold its columns upright" (*Ego fulcio collumnas eius*). The Pillars of Hercules, concludes Cummins, "are no longer the gateway to the New World. The New World now supports the Old, and without it the pillars would collapse" (Cummins 2012: 407–408)[25]. As we move from allegory to fact, America quite literally turns into the pillar of European modernity. The Potosí mine emerges as a powerful image of the rise of the modern world and global economy, and of the interplay between modernity's coloniality of human others and its coloniality of nature. We should not forget that modernity arose from the guts of the earth and was carried on the back of llamas (one of them depicted by Murúa on the mountain's left side along with two miners, one on the left and one on the right), other more-than-humans, and human others.

The endogenous and exogenous inferiorization of Byzantium and America, or the coloniality of human others both home and abroad, goes hand in hand with the coloniality of nature. Episode Two will focus on modernity's

---

[25] See also Benavides (2022: 62).

Figure 3 Martín de Murúa, "Allegorical Image of Potosí," in *Historia del origen, y genealogía real de los reyes ingas del Piru*, f. 141v, 1590, Private Collection (photograph provided by Thomas B. F. Cummins).

coloniality of the more-than-human world to discuss the current ecological crisis as a major consequence of modernity's fixations.

Episode Two: Coloniality of Nature

Like the coloniality of human others, modernity's coloniality of nature would have been severely hampered without the Moderns' notion of progress. In nineteenth-century Argentina, the Pampa was famously identified as barbarism, as were the indigenous peoples living in its vast expanse of fertile grasslands, such as the Pehuenches, Tehuelche, and Mapuche, whereas Buenos Aires represented European(ized) civilization (Sarmiento 2001). The conquest of the "wilderness" and its human others was viewed by the Europhile criollo elites as a civilizing project, a progressive advancement of European civilization over nature and indigenous barbarism.[26] In Argentina, modernity's double coloniality is arguably best shown by the so-called "Conquest of the Desert" (1878–1885), the Argentine government's military campaigns against indigenous peoples in the Pampa and Patagonia. The campaigns, Carolyne Larson explains, sought to control indigenous lands and natural resources, exterminating large numbers of indigenous peoples and displacing many others. According to Argentina's traditional narrative, "the conquest became a catalyst for civilization, a necessary action in the interest of national progress, and the dawn of a white Argentina." In his speech to the Congress on August 14, 1878, President Nicolás Avellaneda claimed that "Argentines could only satisfy their own sense of 'propriety, as a virile people' through 'the conquest, sooner rather than later, by reason or by force, of a handful of savages that destroy our principal wealth and impede us from definitively occupying, in the name of the law, of progress and of our own security, the richest and most fertile territories of the Republic'" (Larson 2020a: 1, 4, 10; Larson 2020b: 20–21, 39). In the colonization of the Pampa and Patagonia there is reflected modernity's coloniality of nature and of human others, argued for as economic and sociocultural progress. The human and natural landscapes of the "desert," a space devoid of civilization, must be conquered for the sake of the modern nation's progress.

Today, the Moderns' fixation with and fetishization of progress has switched the emphasis from knowledge to newness. Progress has become a "perpetual and perhaps never-ending challenge and necessity, the very meaning of 'staying alive and well'" (Bauman 2000: 134), even if its horizon is always out of reach. Like the modern, progress renders itself perpetually outdated and thus we are constantly in need of catching up with the latest modernity. Paradoxically, while our technological modernity is making movement increasingly redundant – think of how we may "experience" the world with a single click, or enjoy a simulated campfire on a hotel lawn, or even venture a tour of the Eiffel Tower, the Egyptian pyramids, the Statue of Liberty, and Venice's Grand Canal on a day out in Las Vegas – that same modernity has turned motion, and with it change and progress, into the economy of modern existence (Kefala 2022: 36–37, 57–60).[27] Good is what comes next, we are told.

Progress, however, even in its most conspicuous form as scientific and technological development, is compromised at least with respect to one of its dimensions, that is, certitude and security. In principle, any "accepted knowledge" in natural sciences can be revised or refuted. Modern science has taken a shift toward acknowledging "the endemically indeterministic nature of the

---

[26] In Spanish America, *criollo* refers to people of European origins who are born and raised in America.

[27] On contemporary tourism, see Ritzer and Liska (1997: 97, 105, 107).

world," the significant role carried out by chance, and "the exceptionality, rather than the normality, of order and equilibrium" (Bauman 2000: 136; Giddens 1991: 177). Even staunch defenders of scientific certitude like Karl Popper recognize that "all science rests upon shifting sand" (Giddens 1991: 39). Technology, through which scientific truths become relevant to society in general, produces as much uncertainty as science does, opening new areas of unpredictability and unreliability, which may make technological society look more like a "house of cards" than a solid edifice (Sarewitz 2013: 304–306).

Technological unpredictability often manifests itself brutally in the realms of safety and security, as in the case of military industrialization, the consequences of which are too well known to be discussed here. Two devastating world wars, two atomic bombings, concentration camps and the Holocaust, chemical and biological warfare, and the threat of nuclear disaster are all as much part of the Enlightenment's legacy as are modernity's most formidable achievements. Herbert Marcuse's bleak conclusion in 1964 was that "Auschwitz continues to haunt, not the memory but the accomplishments of man" (Marcuse 2002: 252). The ecological crisis is yet another proof of technological modernity's inherent unpredictability. The use of fossil fuels required by an economic system geared toward continuous economic growth and capital accumulation has set the wagon of humanity on a collision course with extinction.[28] In 2014, the Fifth Assessment Report of the Intergovernmental Panel on Climate Change (IPCC) identified anthropogenic influence on climate as "clear and growing," with effects seen across all oceans and continents. According to the report, the last three decades have been consecutively warmer at the surface of the Earth compared to any previous decade since the mid nineteenth century and many of the developments seen since the mid twentieth century are "unprecedented over decades to millennia" (IPCC 2014: v, 2). Seven years later, the Sixth IPCC Assessment Report reached the sober conclusion that "many changes due to past and future greenhouse gas emissions are irreversible for centuries to millennia, especially changes in the ocean, ice sheets and global sea level" (IPCC 2021: 21).

I have argued that this anthropogenic crisis, a consequence of modernity's coloniality of nature, is born with Descartes's *cogito*. Among the philosophers who trace modernity's origins in the *cogito* is Martin Heidegger, who nevertheless critiques Descartes's dualism. Heidegger argues that no split is possible

---

[28] Serenella Iovino mentions an interesting reference to extinction in the short story "Petrol Pump" (1974) by Italo Calvino: "The day the earth's crust reabsorbs the cities, this plankton sediment that was humankind will be covered by geological layers of asphalt and cement until in millions of years' time it thickens into oily deposits, on whose behalf we do not know" (Calvino 1995: 175). Calvino's prescient story, notes Iovino, "speaks directly to the Anthropocene, reminding us that one of the legacies of our current ecological predicaments may be the reduction of the *Anthropos* to future fossils" (Iovino 2021: 59–60).

between mind and body, subject and object, as Descartes suggested in his
Meditations on First Philosophy (1641), because they are both tied up with
the notion of *Dasein* (being-in-the-world). The subject cannot be separated from
the external world. "The ego is a res, whose realities are representations"
(Descartes 2008: 15, 19, 32; Heidegger 1982: 16, 126, 161). Heidegger, says
Hubert Dreyfus, "questions the view that experience is always and most basic-
ally a relation between a self-contained subject with mental content (the inner)
and an independent object (the outer)." Although he "does not deny that we
sometimes experience ourselves as conscious subjects relating to objects by
way of intentional states [...], he thinks of this as a derivative and intermittent
condition that presupposes a more fundamental way of being-in-the-world that
cannot be understood in subject/object terms" (Dreyfus 1991: 5). Heidegger's
ultimate aim is to overcome modernity's entrenched dualism (Oldmeadow
2010: 269).

Latour expands on the rejection of dualism. The opposite of "body," he writes,
is not "thought," or "mind," or "soul," or "consciousness," as Descartes and the
Moderns claim, but "death." Not an "extended thing," nor inert matter, the Earth
is "a living 'organism'" composed of interlocking living things, among them
humans (Latour 2021: 92, 94, 97). Latour here draws on the writings of the
biochemist James Lovelock, who argued that living beings are agents who
participate in the processes of creating the chemical and partly the geological
conditions of the Earth. This is the so-called Gaia hypothesis that Lovelock
together with microbiologist Lynn Margulis developed in the late 1960s and
1970s.[29] As a metaphor for the living planet, they chose the name "Gaia," the
ancient Greek personification of the Earth. The biosphere, according to the Gaia
hypothesis, is a "self-regulating entity" capable of keeping the planet healthy
(Latour 2018: 75; Lovelock 1995: xv). This assertion leads Latour to paradoxically affirm that Earth "is not nature but artifice [...]. Earth is not green, it's not
primitive, it's not intact, it's not 'natural'. It's artificial through and through."
Earth is an artifice in the sense that it is the risky product of a mechanism, a system
of living things that has supplied livable conditions, which are now being
destabilized by our actions (Latour 2021: 122–123, 126–127). Meanwhile, in
We Have Never Been Modern (1993) he puts forward a negation of modernity
itself. The separation of the subject from the object, which, in Fredric Jameson's

---

[29] Lovelock and Margulis's Gaia hypothesis has drawn much controversy among scientists. Tim
Lenton explains that, even though this was not their intention, the hypothesis "seemed to imply
a sort of purposive control of the global environment by unconscious organisms. Such teleo-
logical reasoning is out of bounds in science." Lenton argues that what Lovelock was in fact
suggesting was "the idea that a complex system like the Earth can self-regulate automatically,
without any conscious foresight or purpose" (Lenton 2016: 5).

words, "constitutes modernity as such and from which we all allegedly continue to suffer today," never truly happened according to Latour. Modernity has never been inaugurated, "we have never been modern" (Jameson 2002: 43; Latour 1993: 11).

Latour reserves the phrase "New Climatic Regime" for climate change, while Eugene Stoermer and Paul Crutzen famously used the term "Anthropocene" to refer to the geological period whose onset they roughly place in the late eighteenth century, around the invention of the steam engine, even though its beginnings are still debated, with some pushing it back to the start of the Holocene approximately 11,700 years ago (Crutzen and Stoermer 2000; Latour 2017).[30] William Ruddiman, for example, argues that the Anthropocene started thousands of years ago with the Neolithic revolution and the domestication of livestock and crops, which led to the clearance of forests and large-scale use of land, producing large emissions of greenhouse gas (Ruddiman 2013: 46–47, 64–66). However, Ruddiman's early Anthropocene remains controversial, in part because, as Tim Lenton explains, the energy supplies available to pre-industrial people to modify their environment were limited. Most scientists link the onset of the Anthropocene to the dawn of the Industrial Revolution when the use of fossil fuel energy increased greatly humanity's impact on the Earth system. It is the exploitation of fossil fuel energy that prompted a massive increase in the world's population, material consumption, food production, and waste products. Within two centuries, the Earth's population has increased from one billion in 1825 to almost eight billion. The concomitant rise in the production of food to match the population explosion has been driven by the increase in land-use, fossil fuel energy, fertilizers, and herbicides, all with adverse consequences for the Earth system (Lenton 2016: 81–82).

Humanity's influence in geology and ecology has been central since the late eighteenth century, while the global effects of our activities have become abundantly obvious (Crutzen and Stoermer 2000: 17–18). For the first time in our short history, we have become a geophysical force. Crutzen later proposed that the Anthropocene's "golden spike" could be placed around the mid twentieth century, coinciding with nuclear tests and the Great Acceleration, a term referring to the escalation of the impact of human activities on the Earth and the biosphere since 1945. The Anthropocene has placed us in the position of seeing an "end of the world" in the most literal sense of the phrase, as a disastrous change in the physical conditions of the species' existence (Danowski and

---

[30] The term "Anthropocene" is said to have been coined by Stoermer in the 1980s and has been widely employed since the early twenty-first century, thanks to Crutzen who encouraged scientists to use it (Purdy 2015: 1–2).

Viveiros de Castro 2017: 5, 29–30). Much ink has been spilled on the devastating consequences of our fossil-fuel, profit-driven economies to the point where some scholars, including Moore, have proposed the term "Capitalocene" instead of the Anthropocene which "names capitalism as a system of power, profit, and re/production in the web of life" (Moore 2017: 606).

Despite the fact that considerable attention has been rightly paid to fossil fuel energy, we tend to think less of activities like industrial fishing, which depletes our oceans far more than oil spills, while abandoned fishing gear, according to a WWF report, is the deadliest type of marine plastic waste, harming vital sea habitats to the extent that it accounts for nearly half of the Pacific trash vortex (WWF 2020: 4, 10). Meanwhile, open sea bottom trawling, which literally plows the seafloor, was drastically enhanced at the start of the nineteenth century and expanded greatly from the early to mid twentieth century, currently nearing continental-slope areas about a kilometer deep. The large, heavy trawl net, whose bottom consists of a thick metal cable or "footrope," is dragged along the ocean floor, crashing or disrupting everything on its course, thus destroying the ecosystem of the seabed (Syvitski et al. 2019: 105). According to the Global Ocean Commission, the oceans produce nearly half of the oxygen we breathe, while absorbing more than 25 percent of the carbon dioxide that humans emit into the Earth's atmosphere. In fact, the oceans store "more than 90% of the heat trapped in the Earth system by greenhouse gas emissions" (Global Ocean Commission 2014: 5). Within the span of the last three generations alone, 75 percent of the human-induced carbon dioxide emissions occurred, human population grew nearly threefold, and the number of people living in cities increased from about 700 million to 3.7 billion. During the same time, the amount of nitrogen synthesized, primarily for fertilizers, increased by more than 81 million tons, reaching over 85 million, up from less than 4 million in the preceding period. The intensification of agriculture through the use of nitrogenous and phosphorus fertilizers, in fact, is driving our waters toward anoxia, killing fish among other more-than-human beings (Lenton 2016: 84; McNeill and Engelke 2014: 4).

Even though the champions and advocates of the Industrial Revolution did not intentionally mean to modify the climate, says Lenton, we cannot act as if we are unaware of the consequences that our industrial activities have on the Earth's climate. He also concedes that such consequences were not altogether unknown to earlier generations. The Swedish Nobel-laureate physicist Svante Arrhenius documented the impact of fossil fuel on global climate in 1896, predicting that over the next three millennia coal combustion would result in a doubling of carbon dioxide levels in the atmosphere, raising global temperature by about 5°C. Arrhenius reduced this millennial forecast to centuries twelve years later, at a time when the global consumption of coal was significantly higher (Lenton 2016: 87, 117; Lovejoy 2019: 300). Interestingly, he gave a positive spin to his findings. "We would then have some right to indulge in the pleasant belief that our descendants, albeit after many generations, might live under a milder sky and in less barren surroundings than is our lot at present" (in Lovejoy 2019: 300).[31] Arrhenius's discovery was as striking as his northern European bias. With his witty remark, the Swedish physicist does not appear to have given much thought to what a 5°C world would mean to individuals living in other parts of the world already enjoying milder skies.

"How could we deem 'realistic' a project of modernization that has 'forgotten' for two centuries to anticipate the reactions of the terraqueous globe to human actions?", asks Latour. "How could we call 'rationalist' an ideal of civilization guilty of a forecasting error so massive that it prevents parents from leaving an inhabited world to their children?". For Isabelle Stengers, who reminds us of the interconnectedness of the ecological and social crises, this is the advent of barbarism. The depletion of ground water and raw material, pesticide poisoning, pollution, and increasing social inequality are all part of this barbarism (Latour 2018: 66; Stengers 2015: 18).

Scientists are virtually unanimous in predicting a 4°C increase in world temperature by the end of the century if we continue "progressing" in the same direction. Back in 2012, World Bank Group President Jim Yong Kim pondered what such a disastrous scenario may imply: wet regions becoming wetter and dry regions drier, decreased food production possibly increasing malnutrition rates, unusual heat waves, more frequent tropical cyclones of high intensity, water scarcity in many parts of the world, permanent loss of biodiversity, and inundated coastal cities. Kim warned that a 4°C world would be vastly different from the one we live in now, bringing with it new risks and a great deal of uncertainty that would limit our capacity to predict and plan for future adaptation (World Bank 2012: ix).

The World Bank report forecasted climate change implications such as extreme heat waves causing heat-related mortalities, wildfires, crop production losses, the acidification of marine ecosystems with destructive consequences for coral reefs and marine organisms and for people whose livelihoods depend on them, sea-level rise with coastal inundation around the world, intensified rainfall and drought likely leading to increasing mortality, the extinction of species and a transition of the planet's ecosystems into "a state unknown in human experience," further water scarcity in areas of Africa, the Middle East and South Asia as well as crop

---

[31] For excerpts of notes from Arrhenius's lecture at Stockholm University on February 3, 1896, see Rodhe et al. (1997: 4).

yield reductions (e.g., corn and soybeans) threatening global food security, with the poor affected most. Severe floods will hit food production, inducing or heightening nutritional deficits as well as aggravating epidemic diseases. Because of the surge in flooding, contaminants and pathogens could be introduced into healthy water supplies, increasing the frequency of respiratory and diarrheal infections. Warming would in all probability exert a direct influence on several diseases, including vector-borne illnesses like dengue fever and malaria, as well as allergies. Coupled with population growth, climate change will put further strain on the Earth's ecosystem, which is already reaching critical limits. The report added that the anticipated implications on agriculture, water availability, ecosystems, and human health may result in large-scale population relocations as well as in negative consequences for trading systems, the economy, and human security. In a 4°C world, each climate change consequence would trigger a domino effect in other departments. Agricultural production affected by extreme temperatures, for instance, would probably have an impact on our health and livelihoods (World Bank 2012: xiii–xviii). In its bleak predictions, the World Bank ironically eclipsed Marcuse's grim conclusions, as did ten years later the UN Secretary-General António Guterres, who warned that humanity is on the verge of "collective suicide" (in Harvey 2022).

Climate activists, like scientists, have long alerted us to the existential threat that climate change poses to humanity. For Naomi Klein, the only historical counterpart for such a crisis is to be found in the Cold War and the fear of nuclear disaster (Klein 2015: 15). We come across a graphic description of Klein's analogy in Jonathan Schell's essay "The Fate of the Earth: A Republic of Insects and Grass" (1982), according to which a nuclear catastrophe would be followed by the extinction of numerous ocean species, including some at the bottom of the food chain. Among other calamities, it would also bring about a permanent or temporary change of the planet's climate, "with the outside chance of 'dramatic' and 'major' alterations in the structure of the atmosphere; the pollution of the whole ecosphere with oxides of nitrogen [. . .]; the scalding and killing of many crops [. . .] and the attendant risk of global epidemics" (Schell 2000: 93). Schell's republic of insect and grass is a possible high-consequence risk of modernity that may turn out to be no more terrifying than climate crisis. Most nuclear scientists, says Klein, "never told us that we were almost certainly going to put our civilization in peril if we kept going about our daily lives as usual, doing exactly what we were already doing, which is what the climate scientists have been telling us for years." The truth is that even if we stopped emitting carbon dioxide today, many consequences of climate change would continue to occur for centuries, according to the Fifth IPCC Assessment Report (Giddens 1991: 171; IPCC 2014: 16; Klein 2015: 15).

The view that the opportunity for civilization to grow is limitless, is "prehistoric," Marilyn Brown and Benjamin Sovacool write, not least because it goes against even the most basic lessons from biology, ecology, physics, and thermodynamics. Giddens makes a similar observation when he refers to the "development fatigue" experienced by many people in the economically advanced countries, while Latour stresses our economic model's non-objective, unrealistic nature: "How could we accept as 'objective' economic theories that are incapable of integrating into their calculations the scarcity of resources whose exhaustion it had been their mission to predict?" (Brown and Sovacool 2011: 1; Giddens 1991: 166; Latour 2018: 66). Former Senior Economist for the World Bank Herman Daly shares this view. Because the earth is "developing without growing," he reminds us, we must ultimately adapt to "the same behavioral model of development without growth, alias 'sustainable development'" (Daly 1996: 223).

Although capitalism's role in climate change is undisputable, the origins of this anthropogenic, ecological-turned-eschatological crisis can be traced back to Bacon's natural philosophy, whose ultimate goal was dominion and control over nature, and, as noted earlier, to Descartes's dualism. For Bacon, on the one hand, natural philosophy does not aim so much at the pursuit of knowledge as such, but at the restoration of our "sovereignty" over nature, which humans reportedly lost following their expulsion from the Garden of Eden (Gaukroger 2001: 78). "It is not the pleasure of curiosity, nor the quiet of resolution, nor the raising of the spirit, nor victory of wit," he explains, "that are the true ends of knowledge; some of these being more worthy than other, though all inferior or degenerate: but it is a restitution and reinvesting (in great part) of man to the sovereignty and power (for whensoever he shall be able to call the creatures by their true names he shall command them) which he had in his first state of creation" (Bacon 2011: 222). Thanks to Descartes's thinking subject, on the other hand, we have seen that nature becomes natural resources at our disposal. This is the moment of the birth of the ecological crisis or the coloniality of nature, which is inseparably entangled with the coloniality of human others.

Security is tied up with Habermas's other dimensions of progress, that is, happiness and fulfillment, freedom and dignity, and material prosperity, while climate crisis, military industrialization, and socioeconomic disparities all show that modernity's developmentalist logic is troubled in all these areas. Since the mid 1990s, the top one percent of the world's population, according to a 2022 Oxfam report, has seized twenty times more of global wealth than the bottom half. Meanwhile, the world's ten richest men doubled their wealth during the COVID-19 pandemic, when the earnings of the ninety nine percent worsened because of the global health emergency. Two hundred and fifty-two males globally have amassed more wealth than one billion females (women and girls) in Latin

America, the Caribbean, and Africa together, while, on average, twenty of the world's wealthiest billionaires are projected to be emitting about eight thousand times more carbon dioxide than the bottom billion (Oxfam 2022: 7). Similar data are published in the 2022 World Inequality Report, which details that in the period 1820–1910 global inequality increased and remained at a high level and that income inequalities both within countries and between countries were nearly as extensive in 2020 as in 1910. Since 1995 there has been extreme growth at the top to the extent that the overall wealth of the global bottom half is three times smaller than that of the top 0.001 percent, even though the former group is 50,000 times larger than the latter, which in 2021 was represented by just about 51,700 multimillionaires globally (World Inequality Lab 2022: 54, 56, 91).

The interplay between technology and colonialism is well established. Western technology, notes Keld Nielsen, historically set the stage for an extensive and devastating slave trade, while western colonialism was greatly aided by steamships, railways, telegraphs, and, of course, effective rifles, which made possible human and natural exploitation worldwide – what I have called modernity's double coloniality. One of the most significant challenges posed by western technology is due to the vast economic inequalities between different parts of the world that, even though they have access to the same information, do not share the same riches or living standards (Nielsen 2013: 27).

Despite the obvious unsustainable nature of our techno-economic growth model and the resulting social inequalities, the developmentalist logic remains entrenched today. It is now strikingly clear that we have created an untenable way of living. We are already changing the climate, writes Lenton, we are massively speeding land erosion and ocean sedimentation, decreasing ocean oxygen levels while increasing acidity, and eradicating other species at an unparalleled rate. He is no doubt correct in stating that hitting the break on the population explosion by having fewer children will partially help us forge a more sustainable future. After all, nobody had ever told us that extinction may occur not because we are too few, but because we are too many. But Lenton associates the stabilization of the human population with "development," the realization of which, as we now know all too well, has pushed the Earth to and beyond its critical limits. Interestingly, he appears to envision "development" for the so-called "underdeveloped" countries. It is true, he says, that "fertility rates have already fallen below the replacement level in many developed countries. Hence if development is realized globally, we can project a declining human population in the long term" (Lenton 2016: 90, 107, 111).[32]

---

[32] Lenton acknowledges that "development also increases energy and material consumption" and that "the sustainability challenge is not primarily about stabilizing population (although that will help)" (Lenton 2016: 111).

When a natural scientist like Lenton refers to "our" industrial activities, he appears to downplay the fact that not all the modern world's population has had the same impact on the Earth system (Lenton 2016: 117). Many indigenous peoples, although by no means all, have led and continue to lead far more sustainable lifestyles than ours, while, as Déborah Danowski and Eduardo Viveiros de Castro put it, "there are too few people with too much world, and too many people with way too little." The truth is that not all of us have the same share of responsibility in modernity. Ultimately, many indigenous peoples, according to Danowski and Viveiros de Castro, prefer to keep their population relatively stable "instead of increasing 'productivity' and 'improving' technology in order to create conditions ('surplus') so that there can always be more people, more needs." Today, about 370 million traditional indigenous peoples in over seventy countries around the world belong to "collectives that are not recognized" by nation-states, nor do they consider themselves as ordinary citizens of the countries that contain them and frequently divide them (Danowski and Viveiros de Castro 2017: 96–97, 104). It is also worth noting that while accounting for only five percent of the worldwide population, indigenous peoples occupy, use, or own up to twenty two percent of global land, which is home to four fifths of the Earth's biodiversity (UNDP 2011: 54).

Ecological and socioeconomic inequalities between and within countries are intimately intertwined. The top ten percent of carbon emitters, according to the 2022 World Inequality Report, are responsible for nearly half of all emissions, while the bottom fifty percent emits just about twelve percent of the total. Disparities within countries currently account for the majority of global emissions inequality, implying that environmental policies will likely fail if they do not properly take into consideration the extent of inequalities within countries. The report highlights the 2018 Yellow Vest movement in France as an example, which rejected the implementation of the carbon tax because it was not matched by substantial measures to compensate for middle- and low-income households. The reform was put forward concurrently with "a suppression of the progressive wealth tax on financial assets and capital incomes." Most people opposed it because many middle- and low-income households were expected to pay it daily to go to their workplace when not using their cars was not an option for them. Meanwhile, tax cuts were offered to the wealthy who live in cities, where low-carbon transportation options are available, and who additionally enjoy low energy tax rates when traveling by air. What the French example tells us, the report's authors conclude, is that the drastic reduction of greenhouse gas that is urgently needed in wealthy countries can only be achieved if social and ecological inequalities are closely addressed when designing environmental policies. Climate policymakers must factor in not only social and carbon inequalities, but also how different policy measures, such as taxes, regulations, and investments, affect socioeconomic groups differently (World Inequality Lab 2022: 16, 123, 126–129, 131).

Proponents of climate justice remind us that the ecological crisis is associated with unequal capitalist development inflected by gender, race, and class. Speaking of the 2009 report of the United Nations Department of Economic and Social Affairs *Promoting Development and Saving the Planet*, Dipesh Chakrabarty traces the origins of the climate justice debate to the booklet *Global Warming in an Unequal World: A Case of Environmental Colonialism* (1991) by Indian environmental activists Anil Agarwal and Sunita Narain. That work stressed the notion of "common but differentiated responsibilities" as well as the need to consider per capita emissions when discussing greenhouse gases. Chakrabarty points out that countries like India and China, whose energy supplies rely heavily on coal, the cheapest fossil fuel option, justify emissions by citing the sheer number of people who desperately require a route out of poverty (Chakrabarty 2021: 55–57, 59).

Despite his strong social sensibilities, Chakrabarty has been accused of "depoliticizing" climate crisis when embracing the term Anthropocene, which shifts the focus to human agency more generally, diverting attention away from issues of accountability, "the role of capitalism, empires, uneven development, and the drive for capitalist accumulation." A critique of capitalism, he says in his defense, does not suffice when it comes to addressing concerns about our history now that the ecological crisis has been recognized and "the Anthropocene has begun to loom on the horizon of our present." Even though he acknowledges that climate change is intrinsically related to the high-energy geared society dictated by capitalist industrialization, he notes that the ecological crisis has highlighted some other conditions for the presence of human life which are in no way inherently linked to capitalism, socialism, or nationalism. He explains that these conditions are more tied to the history of life on Earth, how different forms of life interact with each other, and how the extinction of a certain species can be detrimental to another. Drawing on recent developments in Earth system science, he adds that regardless of our technological, social, or economic choices, we do not have the luxury of upsetting conditions that serve as "boundary parameters" of our existence and which are "independent of capitalism or socialism." Chakrabarty's conclusion is that current global warming is an example of the so-called planetary warming, which has occurred on several planets, including Earth, with different implications. "It just so happens," he claims, "that the current warming of the earth is primarily a result of human actions" (Chakrabarty 2021: 16, 35–36, 40–41, 75).

Slavoj Žižek is one of Chakrabarty's critics who accuses him of missing the full depth of the dialectical interaction between socioeconomic models of human development and the natural parameters of life on the planet. Although these parameters are undeniably "independent of capitalism and socialism," in other words, they potentially pose a threat to all living beings regardless of our political and economic models, he writes, the fact that they have been destabilized by global capitalism has a more profound implication than Chakrabarty allows. In a way, we must admit that "the fate of the Whole (life on earth) hinges on what goes on in what was formerly one of its parts (the socio-economic mode of production of one of the species on earth)." Therefore, he concludes, we can only address the universal issue of our collective survival on Earth by addressing the particular impasse of capitalism. "The key to the ecological crisis does not reside in ecology as such" (Žižek 2010: 333–334).

Similarly, Peter Wagner points out that, while climate change is a natural phenomenon, as one discovers by studying the planet's deep history, the current ecological crisis is anthropogenic rather than "planetogenic." He also criticizes Chakrabarty for understanding the connection between freedom and energy as something rigid and unalterable, presuming that material well-being and free-dom are inevitably energy intensive. Although Chakrabarty indicates that in their discussions of freedom since the Enlightenment, the Moderns were unaware of the geological force they were obtaining in tandem with their freedom, says Wagner, he nevertheless fails to notice that the contingent invention of a concept of freedom that ignores "its planetary condition of possibility," if this is indeed the case, does not imply that any notion of freedom can be fulfilled solely by "massively increasing the use of biophysical resources." Wagner goes on to cite Ian Baucom who wonders whether we can find other ways to conceive freedom (Wagner 2022: 33–34). In the latter's words, climate change may well be telling us that the Moderns' "great projects of freedom [...] *are* the catastrophes leading [...] to an image of the end metonymically figured not only by the image of a single vanishing species, but by virtually all the tipping-point, threshold-crossing, cascading images of the 4°C world: the image of death, the image of extinction" (Baucom 2014: 140, original emphasis).

The connection between freedom and development recalls Amartya Sen's notion of "development as freedom," which Chakrabarty cites as an example of why the desire of the middle classes outside the West to develop or modernize was not simply driven by utility, greed, or profit (Chakrabarty 2021: 103). Development, Sen famously argued, can be viewed "as a process of expanding the real freedoms that people enjoy" (Sen 2001: 3). Chakrabarty emphasizes that we cannot discuss the politics of climate crisis without considering the ways in which "issues of 'development' affect subaltern modernizers in history." For instance, he criticizes thinkers like Latour for failing to pay enough attention to the relationship between modernization projects introduced by anticolonial modernizers in former colonial territories in Africa, Asia, the Pacific, and other places in the 1950s and 1960s, the aspiration for capitalist progress in countries like China and India today, and the ecological crisis. Latour, he continues, "speaks of 'provincializing modernity' as a European task." Born in Europe and spread to the rest of the world by Europe, in Latour's mind modernity should now be provincialized by European intellectuals like himself; it is they who should "put it back in its proper place" (Chakrabarty 2021: 97, 100–101, 105, 111).

Chakrabarty's criticism is fair. The fact that Europe has not been able to prevent the globe from "turning into the Global," claims Latour, places it in a unique position of responsibility. "It is up to Europe to 'de-globalize' this project and thereby to restore its integrity." Due to its history, Europe "has to plunge in first because it was the first to be responsible" (Latour 2018: 102, 104). This is Latour's thinking but, as Chakrabarty reminds us, modernity's global project acquired "a second and original life in the hands of anticolonial modernizers," whose desire for modernization was far from a copy-paste gesture. Many anticolonial leaders, among them Rabindranath Tagore, Mahatma Gandhi, and Jawaharlal Nehru, renewed and repurposed European debates on modernity as freedom to meet their needs (Chakrabarty 2021: 111, 113). That Chakrabarty has a perfectly valid point here is obvious, but it is also clear that we urgently need to find other ways to conceptualize freedom. We must be able to imagine and forge alternative paths that will help us be(come) free off the beaten path of the Enlightenment's developmentalist logic, which is pushing the planet beyond its tipping points.

Change, says Haraway, "is not the problem; rates and distributions of change are very much the problem." Modernity has brought about what she describes as the inflection point that "changes the name of the 'game' of life on earth for everybody and everything." The inflection point is "more than climate change; it's also extraordinary burdens of toxic chemistry, mining, nuclear pollution, depletion of lakes and rivers under and above ground, ecosystem simplification, vast genocides of people and other critters, et cetera, et cetera, in systemically linked patterns that threaten major system collapse after major system collapse after major system collapse" (Haraway 2016: 73, 100). In the current ecological context, "there are no reliable scaffolds for any living system to hold on to [. . .]. All clocks are lying. All metrics bent" (Maran 2020: 59). Although we know that we, the *Anthropoi*, are to blame, the term "Anthropocene" ultimately shifts responsibility to all humans, including the premoderns and nonmoderns. There is no doubt that negative human impact on Earth predates modernity (this is Ruddiman's early Anthropocene) and that climate change affects us all, living and nonliving things, but there is equally no doubt that the ecological crisis and environmental injustice is the work of the Moderns and their (our) *way of thinking* about humans and more-than-humans. This way of thinking has been historically realized – it has economically, politically, and socially *materialized* – in capitalism and its various reconfigurations since the Industrial Revolution. As a result, from the perspective of many indigenous peoples today, as well as of premodern civilizations like Byzantium and pre-Columbian America, Stoermer's and Crutzen's Anthropocene is a misnomer. Humanities (in Greek *Anthropistikes Spoudes*) and environmental humanities in particular have a critical role to play in the arena of environmental justice and, crucially, in exposing and undoing modernity's double coloniality, in other words, the Modern *Anthropoi*'s way of thinking that led to the Anthropocenic catastrophe.

"Periodical apocalypses" are a staple in indigenous mythologies. Recently, the Mbyá Guaraní in South America have developed an eschatological narrative, according to which the Whites will not be included in the recreation of the Earth and humanity following the catastrophe (Danowski and Viveiros de Castro 2017: 76–77), while the Yanomami living in the Amazon rainforest on the border between Brazil and Venezuela call the Whites "earth eaters." Referring to the gold prospectors, or *garimpeiros*, who invaded their territory in the 1980s, leading to their decimation through the spread of epidemics and contamination with mercury, the Yanomami say that the Whites appear "to want to devour the earth like giant armadillos and peccaries! [. . .] We do not want our forest to die, covered in wounds and the white people's waste. We are angry when they burn its trees, tear up its floor, and soil its rivers." Looking for minerals like gold and cassiterite, the illegal miners are also nicknamed "stone eaters," "metal eaters," or "destroyers of land-forest." For the Yanomami, the minerals and oils that the white people are at pains to extract from the guts of the earth are not foods but "evil and dangerous things, saturated with coughs and fevers, which *Omama* [the Yanomami demiurge] was the only one to know." According to Yanomami cosmology, Omama made sure to bury minerals and oil deep under the surface of the earth to protect them from sickness and for this reason they must be left undisturbed under the forest (Kopenawa and Albert 2013: 263, 265, 280, 282–283, 285, 540–541). For the ecologically compromised generations of the future, the Yanomami trope of the "earth eater" may well stand in for us Moderns.

Sustainable energy, material recycling, and geoengineering or climate engineering, says Lenton, could help us in our struggle for sustainability, although he recognizes that some geoengineering proposals, like Crutzen's idea of continually injecting for several centuries sulphate aerosol particles into the stratosphere to cool the Earth, may create more risks than the ones they are meant to mitigate (Crutzen 2006; Lenton 2016: 107, 111–113, 120–121). The job of scientists like them is obviously to propose ways in which science may aid in working out a sustainable future, or, to use Chakrabarty's less anthropocentric term, a *habitable* future, even if by now we should know that science *alone* cannot solve humanity's problems (Chakrabarty 2021: 83).[33] As Latour mentions, we must learn to re-orient all our innovation, invention, and ingenuity toward mending this machinery of living things that we call Earth and which creates conditions of livability (Latour 2021: 123, 127). Latour "embraces sciences, not Science," observes Haraway. Although the faith in providential technofixes, according to which technology will eventually save its smart, if unruly, children, is, to put it mildly, movingly silly, "it remains important to embrace situated technical projects and their people. They are not the enemy" (Haraway 2016: 3, 41). In other words, while it would be nonsensical, if self-defeating, to deny the essential part that contemporary and future technologies can and *must* have in our fight against climate change, we can no longer hide behind an uncritical optimism that sees science and technology as a *deus ex machina* that will sooner or later fix the ecological mess. We must not forget that no technological cocktail, no geoengineering innovations, no Promethean epiphany or, to use Ailton Krenak's words, no "technical wizardry" will safeguard the future of the Earth's environment and living beings, including us, if we do not manage to overcome modernity's fixation with infinite progress and developmentalism, if we are unable to reconfigure our relation to both our home and our human and more-than-human partners (Krenak 2020: 62). As ecosemioticians like Timo Maran remind us, humanity's future will grow increasingly dependent as much on its ingenuity as on "its dialogue with the nonhuman world" (Maran 2020: 59). Without *that* dialogue, without *that* reconfiguration of our relation to our more-than-human partners, no sustainable model can be ultimately sustainable.

As noted earlier, modernity's rhetoric of certitude and security falters in the face of the uncertainty and unpredictability generated by scientific and technological breakthroughs, as well as the various mishaps brought about by industrialization and technological modernity in general. The COVID-19 pandemic, which put billions of people on lockdown and caused millions of deaths around the world, exposed the cracks in the modern edifice of certitude and security once more. Whether or not the theory that the virus originated in a lab is eventually proven to be correct may be less important than the increased

---

[33] Chakrabarty explains that habitability's "central concern is life – complex, multicellular life, in general – and what makes *that*, not humans alone, sustainable" (Chakrabarty 2021: 83).

likelihood of future health emergencies. Latour describes a highly paradoxical type of universality emerging from this latest global experience – while not being able to permanently free ourselves is a negative development, realizing that we are all "in the same boat" is a favorable one. This "global awareness" is the positive outcome of the Coronavirus pandemic. Using lockdown as a metaphor, he argues that that we, the "terrestrials," are "locked-down," we are "earth-bound," and since we can no longer get away, we must live our lives in a new way, similar to our experience of the lockdown: "Everyone started to live *at home*, but *in a different way*" (Latour 2021: 47, 52–54, original emphasis).

Whether anthropogenic or not, the COVID-19 pandemic, whose infection mortality rate was fortunately considerably lower than that of other contemporary infectious diseases like Ebola or MERS, puts modernity's achievements as well as scientific and technological overoptimism in perspective (Wilder-Smith 2021: 8). For so-called Singularitarians like Ray Kurzweil, we have so far "evolved" through four epochs: Physics and Chemistry ("information in atomic structures"), Biology ("information in DNA"), Brains ("information in neural patterns"), and Technology ("information in hardware and software designs"). Two more epochs await us, Kurzweil tells us, which will bring about the fusion of human and machine. He calls them Merger of Technology and Human Intelligence, and The Universe Wakes Up. The former, which will generate the transition to our singular, posthuman future, is not far away. He anticipates that several decades ahead the fifth epoch will allow "our human-machine civilization" to overcome the constraints of the human brain (Kurzweil 2005: 14–17, 20–21). The envisioned fusion of artificial intelligence and human consciousness, codified into software and "uploaded onto the computer network so as to be available for posterior reincarnation in bodies that are purely synthetic or genetically engineered," will finally herald, we are told, our long-awaited victory over that centuries-old enemy known as death (Danowski and Viveiros de Castro 2017: 46). Why then bother with the ecological crisis if we are becoming posthuman? Apart from the fact that by now we should be wary of messianic narratives of unlimited progress, Singularitarians like Kurzweil do not appear to be too concerned that the ailing planet may not be able "to grant us enough time for the leap ahead." The ecological crisis is not factored into their calculations (Danowski and Viveiros de Castro 2017: 47). Climate change, a consequence of modernity's coloniality of nature, may prove to be a most powerful indictment of a self-congratulating modernity, which has projected per-petual newness and boundless progress as the panacea for all the woes that afflicted premodern and nonmodern societies like Byzantium and pre-Columbian America, themselves victims of modernity's coloniality of human others. "Exodus: Beyond Modernity" will return to the Moderns' fixation with the "new" and the systemic crises of the "modern" in order to speculate on modernity's possible futures.

Exodus: Beyond Modernity

Episodes One and Two have discussed modernity's double coloniality: the coloniality of human others and the coloniality of nature. The Moderns' colonial gaze objectified both human others like Byzantium and indigenous America and the more-than-human world. For modernity, says Val Plumwood, nature "encompasses the underside of rationalist dualisms that oppose reason to nature, mind to body [...], human to animal [...]. Progress is the progressive overcoming, or control of, this 'barbarian' non-human or semi-human sphere by the rational sphere of European culture and 'modernity'" (Plumwood 2003: 52–53). The Moderns regarded many indigenous peoples as primitive and childish, closer to nature than civilization, to animal than human. As colonized human others in America and other European colonies around the world were often viewed as "part of nature," they were "treated instrumentally as animals" (Huggan and Tiffin 2015: 6).[34] Meanwhile, Byzantium, like nature, is seen as inert, a gigantic tank of readily available knowledge. Thanks to the bequest of those "librarians of humanity," the purportedly limitless supply of natural resources, and the material and epistemic wealth of indigenous America, among others, the Moderns thought they could drive a prodigious new epoch of intellectual maturity and endless progress into an inevitable and never-ending future. The fixation with "newness" that still enchants contemporary society, in which terms like "modern" and "progress" have become classics, speaks of the strong currency of modernity's legacy and so does the afterlife of Byzantium in the western imagination. The latter, we have seen, reflects the persistence of the irrational myth of modernity at home.

If we have not gone anywhere past modernity's logic, despite the shift from Fordist capitalism to globalization and specialized markets, or, in Bauman's words, from "solid"/"hardware" modernity to "liquid"/"software" modernity (Bauman 2000: 25, 113, 116), then we still necessarily speak from *within* modernity's conceptual and epistemological systems. Our high modernity may put aspects of the "modern" into crisis, but it nevertheless continues to adhere to many others. "Global civilization," say Danowski and Viveiros de Castro, is the "arrogant name" we use to refer to the global expansion of a capitalist economic model driven by fossil fuel energy (Danowski and Viveiros de Castro 2017: 9). There is no doubt that we are still within the contours of modernity.

---

[34] In recent years, there has been a synergy between postcolonial critique and ecocriticism, what Cara Cilano and Elizabeth DeLoughrey have referred to as "postcolonial ecocriticism" (Cilano and Loughrey 2007). For a succinct account of the different manifestations of postcolonial ecocriticism, see Huggan and Tiffin (2015: 1–26). If, according to decolonial thinkers like Quijano, we are far from inhabiting a *post*-colonial world, that is, a world free from the logic of coloniality which remains rampant in contemporary global capitalism (Quijano 2000: 342), the term "decolonial ecocriticism" may be more appropriate.

Far from being monolectic, the "modern" has always been rife with contradictions. It would be myopic, naïve, and unhistorical to refute modernity's spectacular accomplishments in so many spheres of our existence. Equally naïve would be to believe that alternative historical paths would have been – or were – free of inherent antinomies and fallacies. But acknowledging modernity's crucial contributions does not mean that we should remain locked up in its rhetoric of exceptionalism, its assumed historical inevitability, its fixation with newness, its colonial visions, and its systemic crises, which have increasingly put humanity under strain and pushed the planet to its critical limits.

Modernity adopts a solipsistic attitude toward what it views as external to itself both in time and space, despite the fact that endogenous and exogenous histories have been constitutive of the "modern." The name "modern," in fact, reveals this solipsism by monopolizing Hebe's eternal youth and perpetual newness. But in a gesture similar to that of calling "Byzantine" the people who called themselves Romans or describing their millennial history as "worthless" and regressive, our modernity, which has barely run half the time span of the Eastern Roman Empire, will sooner or later become tomorrow's antiquity, perhaps a proto-digital antiquity, which is a far more positive term than Henri Lefebvre's "period of nihilism" or the Yanomami's "earth eaters" (Lefebvre 1995: 224). Whatever future generations will call us, there is little doubt that modernity will be remembered as one of humanity's most arrogant epochs.

With the *cogito*, notes Frédérique Apffel-Marglin, "the mind also departed from matter, transmuting the body and the world into soulless mechanisms, transforming us into the only observers of an inert material reality." As a result of the subject/object split, "the powers and wealth of this world became voiceless, bereft of their old agency." We learned to call them "natural resources," or things without agency, existing solely for our benefit (Apffel-Marglin 2011: 4). At the same time, modernity's reifying processes, emanating from Descartes's subjectivity, have impacted not only the Earth's environment and more-than-human living beings, but also the modern human beings. Cartesian subjectivity has made (at least some of) us the "masters and possessors of Nature" (Descartes 2006: 51), as well as the masters and possessors of other human beings. In modernity, more-than-humans and human others are bound together by coloniality. While modernity turns the planet into natural resources, the subject-turned-object becomes "human resources," and growth, singled out as progress, "continues to impose itself as the only conceivable horizon" (Stengers 2015: 20). Almost everything now seems to be reified and for sale, including former adversaries like tradition, which is being repackaged as one of the priciest goods of the latest modernity, seen, for example, in sanitized versions of agritourism, alternative medicine business, retro clothing, and the organic product industry.

As the current maxim goes, it is easier to imagine the end of the world than the end of capitalism, but as Pittacus of Mytilene's (c. 640–568 BCE) older saying has it, "against necessity not even the gods fight" (in Campbell 1991: 436–437). The ecological crisis, which is driving a self-defeating modernity progressively out of control, already appears to be our Trojan horse. As a result, the question of where modernity is bound for emerges. We can only speculate, of course, but the next "modernity" may unavoidably have to be a radical departure from Cartesian solipsism, a new historical and epistemological break and a paradigm shift that would move the focus from an anthropocentric to a cosmocentric or ecocentric economy, now emerging as the new categorical imperative. To start, the verb *modernize*, writes Latour, should be substituted in our lexicon with *ecologize* (Latour 2013: 99). Indigenous movement leaders like Krenak, for whom "everything is nature," agree with this view. For a long time, he says, we were told that we human beings "stand apart from the great big organism of Earth, and we began to think of ourselves as one thing, and Earth another: Humankind *versus* Earth." But as we cannot "peel ourselves off the earth," it is time "we abandon our anthropocentrism" (Krenak 2020: 5–6, 27).

Cosmocentrism should not be interpreted as anti-human. Contrary to Hebrew cosmogony, in several indigenous American cosmologies humans are placed at the beginning of Creation, not at the end. Many indigenous myths refer to a primeval humanity, which, as Danowski and Viveiros de Castro clarify, was either created by a demiurge or simply pre-existed everything and was used to fashion the world. "This primordial humankind," they note, "progressively changed, either spontaneously or, again, under the action of a demiurge, into the biological species, geographical features, meteorological phenomena, and celestial bodies that compose the present cosmos." Humankind is the only part that remained the same and is the primary matter of all living forms. Those indigenous peoples who consider more-than-human living beings as ex-humans, they conclude, "have never been modern, as they have never had a Nature that they either have lost or needed to liberate themselves from" (Danowski and Viveiros de Castro 2017: 63–64, 67, 69).

Naturally, it would be a mistake to believe that *all* indigenous peoples around the world have historically embraced or, even less so, continue to embrace the same ecological model. In no way should we assume a past and/or contemporary indigenous ecological universality. Homogenizing the ecological attitudes of heterogeneous groups of peoples even at a given moment in time, let alone diachronically, is fraught with problems, as is, in fact, the use of the term "indigenous," which is awkwardly used (including in this Element) to refer to people who would rarely identify with it – instead, they would call themselves Krenak, Mapuche, Potawatomi, Tehuelche, Yanomami, and so on. Equally problematic would be to make an essentializing claim about indigenous earth-reverence, attributing ecological wisdom to all things indigenous. It would also be *unhistorical* to think of indigenous peoples merely as victims or bystanders of modernity in a world where there is scarcely "a pure outside, untouched by the modern" (Escobar 2007: 186).[35] Contact with modernity cannot be understood in solely negative or positive terms, just as modernity itself is not monolectic. However, based on evidence spanning more than ten thousand years, the prevalent principles underpinning the relationship that many indigenous peoples historically developed with the Earth's environment and other living beings, according to Dan Shilling, were "*restraint* and *reverence* – restraint because, as people close to the land, they understood and embraced their dependence on Earth resources; reverence because all was a gift from the Creator, whose animated universe meant animals, trees, and rocks were another 'people'" (Shilling 2018: 12). Although not all indigenous people embrace this view today, some of them do. A member of the Potawatomi people, Kyle Whyte tells us that the Anishinaabe of North America use the verb *bimaadizi*, or "living in a good and respectful way," to refer to their "integrated conception of life," which involves, among others, inter- and intra-generational social and cultural relationships as well as "the intimacy of human relations with plants, animals, and entities" (Whyte 2018: 58).

Drawing on Tim Ingold's essay "An Anthropologist Looks at Biology" (1990), Stefano Varese explains that cosmocentrism seeks to transcend the binary culture/nature embedded in modernity's anthropocentric rationalism by repositioning the human being within the totality of life. He argues that we owe the distinction between *nomos* (law, custom) and *phusis* (nature) to the pre-Socratic philosophers and the humanization of nature to Aristotle, while he understands western science as calculative and the product of Renaissance humanism, Cartesian rationalism, and enlightened thinking. Varese projects the contemplative attitude, which according to Rodolfo Kusch prevails in indigenous American thinking, against the calculative thinking of western capitalism, pointing out that many indigenous societies are imbued with a "sacramental logic of place." They regard the environment "as part of the

---

[35] Christopher Nowlin, for instance, highlights the case of increasing indigenous participation in "industrial-scale development projects" led by non-indigenous capitalists in Canada. Although "some level of continued industrial development is likely required to lift some Indigenous communities from poverty today," Nowlin argues, "the proposition that billion or multi-million-dollar scales of Indigenous participation in oil and gas industries are needed for this purpose stretches credulity" (Nowlin 2021: 1, 96).

cosmic landscape" and emphasize "topos" over "logos." Rather than favoring humans over nature, he writes, such contemplative thinking puts forward a cosmocentric or polycentric view of the world resting on the logic of diversity and reciprocity: "What I take from the earth, the world, nature, must be returned." His observation that diversity and reciprocity informed the epistemic and moral systems of the indigenous peoples of America for millennia makes him speak of "a culture of moral ecology" that understands nature "as a good of limited use and regulated not only by human decisions, but by a cosmic pact involving the entire living universe" (Kusch 2010: 5; Varese 2011: 101, 104, 115–118).

Apffel-Marglin borrows the term "cosmocentric" from Varese to replace the widely used concept of "gift economy" in anthropology with that of "cosmocentric economy," which she defines as "a radically non-anthropocentric type of economy," one that is fundamentally different from the utterly anthropocentric economy of capitalism. She finds in cosmocentrism "a regenerative, non-exploitative economy" governed by the principles of redistribution and reciprocity among humans, more-than-humans, and "aspects of the cosmos" which, she argues, create equity as opposed to uneven distribution of wealth and secure "the regeneration of the sources of livelihood for humans" (Apffel-Marglin 2012: 16–18).

Even if some might accuse anthropologists like Varese and Apffel-Marglin of idealizing indigenous cosmocentric economies, cosmocentrism may paradoxically constitute a new humanism in the context of the current ecological crisis, which has shifted focus from *living well* to *surviving*.[36] "We are faced with an unforeseen astrological conjuncture, from which we are unable to calculate a horoscope," Lefebvre remarked in 1962, alluding to modern society's "great challenge" to outshine nihilism (Lefebvre 1995: 224). This challenge may ultimately be *post-socialist* as well as *post-capitalist*, a third way allowing us to cut loose from modernity's double coloniality. Such a *cosmocentric* turn should not be interpreted as a return to a rhapsodized premodern past, a mere privileging of indigenous or other perspectives, nor as a ready-made solution extracted from the past and exported to the future. As Latour argues, we can certainly "relearn the old recipes," rethink ancient wisdom, and "learn from the few cultures that have not yet been modernized." But we should not fool

---

[36] Speaking from the viewpoint of "critical posthumanism," Rosi Braidotti has argued for a "Zoe-centred egalitarianism," which she sees as "the core of the post-anthropocentric turn." She states that a "zoe-centred," or life-centered, "approach connects human to non-human life so as to develop a comprehensive eco-philosophy of becoming." Her conclusion is that "there is a necessary link between critical posthumanism and the move beyond anthropocentrism," which she defines "as expanding the notion of Life towards the non-human or *zoe*" (Braidotti 2013: 50, 60, 104).

"ourselves with illusions: for them, too, there is no precedent." In the history of humanity, no society has been forced "to grapple with the reactions of the earth system to the actions of eight or nine billion humans" (Latour 2018: 44).

The cosmocentric turn should not necessarily be taken as a revival of pantheistic or animistic notions of the world either. Instead, it should be viewed as a vital break with modernity's solipsism, a reconfiguration of our relation to the cosmos that surrounds us and whose survival is entangled with ours. Such reciprocity could bring about a true *post*-modern transition, taking us beyond the economy of modernity and into what we might term postmodern *ecologics*.[37] What I have in mind is an *ecological thinking* (logics/logos) that would impel us to reconceptualize the ways in which we manage (economics) our home planet (*oikos*). Contrary to Jean-François Lyotard's "postmodernity," defined by him as the death of grand narratives and understood by theoreticians like Giddens as "a shift away from [...] faith in humanly engineered progress," such a *post*-modernity would do exactly the opposite (Giddens 1991: 2; Lyotard 1984). It would liberate progress from the tyranny of the modern, enabling us to forge ahead and beyond modernity toward procuring our shared future on the planet. A consequence of modernity in many ways, cosmocentrism may be a new grand narrative, but one that would nevertheless concern the long-term survival of human and more-than-human beings on Earth. After all, as Krenak puts it, "the earth has had countless other configurations, many of them without us on it, so why is it that we cling so stubbornly to this idea of the earth as humanity's backyard?". The misguided belief that we have always related to the planet the way we do now is "the deepest mark the Anthropocene has left" (Krenak 2020: 58).

Living with Gaia, or perhaps for a change with Pachamama and Papatūānuku, the Andean and Māori figures of Mother Earth, involves adapting to the changing conditions in a way that would allow us to continue existing while mitigating the crisis. For some this is hardly a new story. Many native peoples around the world have been and are still forced to adapt to their shifting environments because of human- and nature-induced changes. Indigenous peoples, in fact, often stress that the environment in which they live has always been subject to change, making them more confident in their ability to adjust to the effects of climate change (Nakashima et al. 2018: 9). Such a case are the Yolngu people who live in Australia's northeast Arnhem Land region. Their holistic knowledge system, says Marcus Barber, involves elements that we

---

[37] The term "ecologics" has been used independently by Hanjo Berressem in relation to "Deleuzian ecology." According to Berressem, Deleuze's "radical philosophy [...] conceptualizes humans as radically immanent to a productive, machinic field made up of what is commonly differentiated into 'natural' and 'artificial' machines; a differentiation that Deleuze's philosophy in actual fact undoes because it considers nature as itself artificial" (Berressem 2009: 57–58).

might classify as environmental (e.g., geographic, climatic, meteorological, and ecological) and includes a "sophisticated understanding of coastal water cycles." The Yolngu believe that "to live safely, people must not only have knowledge of the country, they must also be known by it and by the ancestral beings that created it and still live there." Barber notes that these people have had to develop novel types of knowledge and "new kinds of accommodations with the ancestors and with the places they inhabit" as a response to continuing challenges posed by colonialism and capitalism. Anthropogenic climate crisis naturally presents itself as an extra challenge, which requires both government-led responses as well as further adaptation by the Yolngu to safeguard their survival. But their accumulated knowledge and adaptive capacity, writes Barber citing the words of a Yolngu man, gives them confidence about their ability "to negotiate possible futures" in the face of climate crisis. "Yolngu have been here for 50,000 years and we have survived many changes in the past. It is going to affect you guys, not me. Because I've done it in the past" (Barber 2018: 106, 119). In his study of the environmental knowledge and adaptive capacity of the indigenous communities of the Torres Islands in the Vanuatu archipelago, Carlos Mondragón similarly observes that they "appear to be far more likely to successfully adapt to abrupt climate change than the encompassing, global-ized societies and institutions that are seeking to help them in this process of environmental crisis and transition" (Mondragón 2018: 23, 38).

Far from being "static," a term, we have seen, closely associated with the coloniality of human others and their epistemic systems (let us not forget Byzantium), indigenous or traditional knowledge systems are cumulative and highly adaptive. The Fifth IPCC Assessment Report recognizes that indigenous, traditional, and local practices and knowledge, including the holistic vision of environment and community held by various indigenous peoples, constitute "a major resource for adapting to climate change." Nonetheless, we have not used these situated knowledge systems consistently in our efforts to adapt to the new climatic regime. Integrating them with current practices, the report concludes, "increases the effectiveness of adaptation" (IPCC 2014: 19). Even though climate crisis is a global phenomenon, Igor Krupnik, Jennifer Rubis, and Douglas Nakashima remind us that we experience its impacts at a local level. No matter what the response of humanity as a whole may be, it is important to remember that it will most certainly consist of the aggregate of regional and local actions, as has been the case in the past. Sooner than later environmental agencies and climate scientists will have to "translate their large-scale global and regional scenarios into real-life, high-confidence local models and plans." When this happens, the know-how and "high-resolution 'lenses' of world's indigenous peoples will offer an authoritative template and a philosophy to follow." That philosophy, the authors argue, will increasingly focus on aspects of specific ecosystems, grass-roots projects, local adaptation, spiritual and emotional well-being, and self-reliance, all of which are "trademarks of indigenous peoples' knowledge systems." They also point out that historically many indigenous peoples considered themselves responsible for the well-being of their habitats in a social, spiritual, and practical sense, something which environmental activists have referred to as "ecosystem stewardship," suggesting that this approach should be "promoted to the level of 'planetary' (or Earth) stewardship" defined as a "social-ecological framework for sustaining life in a rapidly changing world" (Chapin et al. 2011: 44–45; Krupnik et al. 2018: 280–282). The word *kaitiakitanga* of the Māori of Aotearoa, New Zealand, for example, refers to environmental stewardship as an ethic of relational and reciprocal guardianship (Wolfgramm et al. 2018: 215–216). The Māori guardian, explains Melissa Nelson citing Jay T. Johnson, "invests his *mana* into the preservation of the resource and in turn derives from the resource *mana*, spiritual life and food to feed his or her community" (Nelson 2018: 252).[38]

That indigenous knowledge systems, also referred to as Traditional Ecological Knowledge and Native Science, should play an important role in adapting to and mitigating climate change should by now be self-evident. After all, it is no coincidence that four fifths of the earth's biodiversity, as we have seen, is currently crammed into one fifth of the world's land occupied, used, or owned by indigenous peoples, who have the smallest ecological footprint. Equally self-evident is the fact that we require far more than indigenous and other traditional experiential know-how. We need to decommodify the Earth and re-establish what Aldo Leopold called an "ethical relation to land," which was practiced by many premodern and nonmodern societies, and still is by some indigenous peoples today (Leopold 2001: 189). A Syilx Okanagan, Jeannette Armstrong writes that historically the Syilx in North America adopted a regenerative approach to the lands they used as a result of "a society-wide environmental ethic based in *ecological knowledge*." She explains that the Syilx

---

[38] Interestingly, Veronica della Dora traces a notion of stewardship in the Byzantine spatial imagination, according to which the *cosmos* as a "manifestation of God" was an interconnected "organic whole." Her reading of Byzantine perceptions of physical and imaginary places questions "cliched narratives of 'Judaeo-Christianity' as the root of modern separation from and exploitation of nature that populate contemporary geography and environmental history books." She argues that "read through patristic, rather than western modern eyes, Genesis is not about domination, but rather stewardship of creation. According to the Greek Church Fathers, humans were hybrid compounds of soul and earthly matter, 'temporal yet immortal, visible yet intelligible', finite yet infinite. [...] As such, the human subject was ultimately not a distanced gazer and greedy exploiter, but the supreme mediator between heaven and earth" (Della Dora 2016: 26, 258–259).

word *tmix^w*, which makes reference "to the ecology of land, including all life forms of a place, consisting of many relationships," is telling of the Syilx notion of human responsibility toward nature. When seen as *tmix^w*, nature becomes "a life force," while humans are viewed as a "single strand of that life force." Syilx *tmix^w-centric* philosophy is characterized by egalitarianism toward all forms of life, an environmental ethic that makes humans stewards of the environment and ensures the regenerative capacity of the land (Armstrong 2018: 96–97, 105, 107, original emphasis). At the other end of the Americas, the Krenak refer to the Doce River in southeast Brazil as "Watu," meaning "grandfather." They see the river as a person rather than a resource. The name *Krenak* itself is a composite of *kre*, or "head," and *nak*, "or land" – headland. Like most indigenous peoples, the Krenak cannot perceive themselves as separate from their land (Krenak 2020: 43, 49).

Dennis Martinez and Enrique Salmon coined the term "kincentric ecology," an "ethical-economic model" which involves a "way of relating respectfully to all life as kin and the earth as a nurturing mother." Kincentricity, explains Martinez, refers to an original pact mentioned in indigenous stories, which underlines reciprocity between humans and animals. According to this primary pact, the latter would offer themselves to the former "provided that humans would take care of the plants and animals by asking permission to harvest – leaving gifts in exchange for lives taken, not taking more than is needed, showing respect for their bodily remains after they were killed and butchered for food, and not failing to regularly care for their habitats and relations." Such a familial relationship between humans and more-than-humans stands in stark opposition to Descartes's dualism and the modern concept of continual growth. Speaking from the viewpoint of kincentric ecology, Martinez considers the environmental solutions of global capitalism, which depend on technological innovations and "'green' capital investments," a conundrum because they are driven by the same economic model, system of values, and way of thinking that created the problem. Curbing the ecological crisis, he argues, is impossible in the current economic conjuncture, which is dominated by consumerism and the individualistic capitalism of the free market, whose survival hinges on continuous expansion (Martinez 2018: 140–141, 147–149; Salmon 2000). Krenak similarly shuns the notion of corporate sustainability. He calls it a "myth invented by corporations to justify their theft of our idea of nature." It is deceitful to use the term sustainability "when we're on the verge of being expelled from Gaia," he writes, adding that "not even the Indigenous communities are sustainable today, because we can't provide for all our needs in a way that is fully integrated with the land." We simply take more than we give back, we are in debt to the planet. "Our deficit to Gaia is half an earth per year" (Krenak 2020: 20–21).

If sustainability is not enough, then what is? For Nelson, it is stewardship and kinship that are fundamental to our collective survival because in the kincentric world human life is intimately interwoven with the more-than-human world. "The natural world has eyes and teeth – it is alive, can see us, and, if ignored, can harm us" (Nelson 2018: 252, 255). Native Science, says Gregory Cajete, a member of the Tewa Pueblo group in New Mexico, reflects an ancient knowledge of relating to the world that is still alive in many indigenous communities. Because we Moderns have lost our "orientations" to our roots and nature, we urgently need to recover and apply it in the current global setting. The ecological crisis requires that the modern mind once again "reestablishes the basis of human awareness in the larger ecology of the world." His conclusion that we live in "the time of the '*rise of the Indigenous mind*'" coincides with that of Danowski and Viveiros de Castro. Even though it may be historically impossible "to go back to being indigenous," they write, "it is perfectly possible – more than that, this is actually taking place – to experience a *becoming-indigenous*" (Cajete 2018: 15–17; Danowski and Viveiros de Castro 2017: 122, original emphasis). As Armstrong puts it citing the Seneca Iroquois historian John Mohawk, it is not so much about specific indigenous peoples from particular locations, but about "re-indigenizing the peoples of the planet" (Armstrong 2018: 106).

To re-indigenize our mind is to rid ourselves of modernity's fixations and decolonize our epistemic systems and mode of thinking, substituting the "monoculture of scientific knowledge" with an "ecology of knowledges." According to Boaventura de Sousa Santos, João Arriscado Nunes, and Maria Paula Meneses, we need to reconfigure the way in which modern scientific knowledge relates to other types of knowledge. Embracing an ecology of knowledges would mean to allow into the context of dominant scientific knowledge different epistemic systems, including native, non-scientific knowledge. Giving equal opportunities to alternative epistemic systems and decolonizing knowledge is key not only in curbing climate change, but also in shaping a fairer society, considering that our current ecological and social crises are so inextricably interconnected (Sousa Santos et al. 2008: xx, xlix). This calls to mind the conclusion that Allen draws when she reads the work of second and third generation theorists of the Frankfurt School like Habermas, Alex Honneth, and Rainer Forst. We need to be open to "the very real possibility of unlearning," she posits, explaining that this is different from Habermas's theory of modernity as an "unfinished project," which forces us Moderns to think that our way of life is "developmentally superior" compared to those we call nonmodern or premodern, even if, in principle, we are willing to be shown incorrect, albeit in a conversation that is carried out "on our own terms."[39] She stresses that we should be ready to engage in an intercultural dialogue with the subaltern without assuming that we know the result of that dialogue from the start. And we must accept that in that process we might be profoundly transformed and that in the future, we might view this transformation of ours "as a kind of progress" (Allen 2017: 201–202). Unlearning is crucial to epistemic decolonization. We must unlearn how we see nature, just as we must unlearn how we see Byzantium – as inert and as repositories of resources. "Learning to unlearn" is "the first step in the grammar of decolonization," notes Walter Mignolo, who borrows the phrase from a 2002 presentation by Jorge García and Luis Macas of the strategic aim of Ecuador's Intercultural University of Indigenous Nationalities and Peoples "Amawtay Wasi" (Mignolo 2007: 485, 510). Allen draws on Mignolo as well as on Linda Martín Alcoff, who argues against Hegel's "epistemology of imperialism." If Hegel, observes Alcoff, has rightly recognized that "all knowledge is perspectival," for him not all perspectives are equal. We Moderns need to root out this "authoritarian perspectivism" which is typical of the Enlightenment, grapple with the cultural and social situatedness of knowledge, and open up to an honest and much needed non-Eurocentric dialogue with epistemic systems other than ours (Alcoff 1996: 205–206; Allen 2017: 209, 213).

Cosmocentrism, or *Gaiocentrism*, could show us ways out of the Anthropocene, ways that could help us sustain the livability of all species. In contrast to the *geocentrism* of the ancients, who lacked our current knowledge of the cosmos, *Gaiocentrism* emerges from the newly acquired knowledge that we Moderns have "to come down to earth" (Latour 2018: 2). Ironically, we have obtained this knowledge after entering the new climatic regime, itself a consequence of our apparent lack of knowledge of the Earth (system), even if most ancients and nonmoderns, like many indigenous peoples, admittedly never lacked such knowledge.

Haraway has suggested the term Chthulucene (*chthon*, earth and *kainos*, new) in response to the Anthropocene and Capitalocene. In the Chthulucene, she tells us, we must learn to "stay with the trouble," to live with Stengers's Gaia as "maker and destroyer," as "an intrusive event that undoes thinking as usual"

---

[39] In his famous 1980 lecture "Modernity: An Unfinished Project," Habermas posed the question whether we should "hold on to the *intentions* of the Enlightenment, feeble as they may be," or if we should "declare the entire project of modernity a lost cause." His well-known response was that "the project of modernity has not yet been fulfilled." More recently, Habermas has acknowledged the importance of an intercultural dialogue in which there should be "mutual perspective-taking." The West constitutes just one participant among many and, like all participants, should be readily open "to be enlightened by others" about its own "blind spots" (Habermas 1981: 9, 12; Habermas 2010).

(Hawaway 2016: 43–44). Stengers's Gaia is different to Latour's. For her Gaia is not a word that stands for harmony and belonging, but for intrusion and ills. It is a "call to resist the Anthropocene, that is, to learn to live with(in) it and against it, which is also to say, *against ourselves*" (Danowski and Viveiros de Castro 2017: 109, 111). After all, some of the changes we have set in motion are either irreversible, such as the extinction of several species, or long lasting. We may be complaining, says Krenak, but we must not forget that "the world we have was made to order. It arrived gift-wrapped and labelled 'non-returnable once opened'. We've been waiting two hundred, three hundred years for just this world, and now all these people are moping and moaning: [...] What sort of world are you boxing and wrapping for future generations?" (Krenak 2020: 66). Lenton gives us a glimpse into what that future world may hold. The most recent example of naturally induced global warming in the history of the Earth was probably prompted by "a volcanic intrusion into ancient fossil fuel reserves and supplemented by the destabilization of frozen methane hydrates under ocean sediments" about 55.8 million years ago. This led to the increase of global temperature by about 5°C. It is estimated that it took about two hundred thousand years for the climate and carbon cycle to fully recover (Lenton 2016: 51). Humanity clearly needs to change its attitude toward spaceship Earth, says the astrophysicist Stamatios Krimigis, because "there is no Noah's Ark to take us to live on other planets" (in Ioannides 2022).

To do this, we must learn to "think-with," to find ways to reconnect with the multiple species of the Earth. Contrary to the Capitalocene and Anthropocene, Haraway emphasizes that in the Chthulucene we humans are not the only important agents, with the other living beings only able to react. All living beings have arisen and survived in the company of microorganisms like archaea and bacteria. Among the examples she mentions is a 2012 paper by Scott Gilbert, Jan Sapp, and Alfred Tauber which bears the Latourian title "A Symbiotic View of Life: We Have Never Been Individuals" (Haraway 2016: 40, 50–51, 55, 64, 67). There the authors challenge the notion of "biological individual," which is key to studies of evolution, development, immunology, physiology, anatomy, and genetics, and instead argue that based on physiological and anatomical criteria, animals (including humans) cannot be classified as individuals because a wide range of symbionts are present and active "in completing metabolic pathways and serving other physiological functions." New evidence in fact shows that without symbionts "animal development is incomplete." They add that "symbionts also constitute a second mode of genetic inheritance, providing selectable genetic variation for natural selection. The immune system also develops, in part, in dialogue with symbionts and thereby functions as a mechanism for integrating microbes into the animal-cell community" (Gilbert et al. 2012: 325–326). It is important that such research on complex biological systems emerges now, concludes Haraway, "when the arts for living on a damaged planet demand sympoietic thinking and action."[40] It may help us realize that "we are humus, not Homo, not anthropos," that is, we are "with and of the earth," and that "the biotic and abiotic powers of this earth are the main story," not us (Haraway 2016: 55, 67). In the eyes of *that* post-modernity which we may or may not call the Chthulucene, our high or liquid modernity already appears as a new abyss of darkness, rather than the heir of an enlightened society and a hothouse of epistemic conquests. Modernity is already becoming the Earth's "Middle Ages" and this, I borrow Haraway's words, "will be written into earth's rocky strata, indeed already is written into earth's mineralized layers" (Haraway 2016: 102). Even a partial awareness of how we are intricately entangled with the more-than-human world, says Louise Westling, may enable "enough humans to find survivable ways to adapt and redirect their cultural behaviors so that we and our biosphere companions can continue to live. Mars is not really an option" (Westling 2022: 59).

From within the confines of our global capitalist society, a cosmocentric or Gaiocentric economy surely looks improbable, if naïvely entertaining, but history has taught us that humanity advances by necessity, the mother of invention and change. Based on the "ontology of the present," this might be a possible "archaeology of the future," which could replenish the depleted tanks of the idea of progress by reconfiguring its content (Jameson 2002: 214–215). No longer a Eurocentric universal narrative of human advancement, progress (if we really must hold onto this term) should be liberated from the fixations of the Enlightenment, embrace its social and cultural situatedness, and acknowledge its plurality across time and space. Modernity's logic of coloniality should give way to ecologics. In the current conjunction of climate crisis and an impending nuclear threat, Theodor Adorno's famous understanding of progress resonates more than ever. "Progress today," he wrote in 1965, "really does mean simply the prevention and avoidance of total catastrophe" (Adorno 2006: 143).

In the late fifth century BCE, Choerilos, a minor poet from the island of Samos in the eastern Aegean Sea, deplored the end of art. "Now, when everything has been portioned out and the arts have reached their limits," he moaned, "we are left behind in the race, and one looks everywhere in vain for a place to drive one's newly yoked chariot" (in Hopkinson 1999: 1). Those who oppose the concept of aesthetic or artistic progress would perhaps argue that literature has barely advanced since the *Epic of Gilgamesh* or Homer's time, let alone Choerilos's, but few would deny the countless permutations it has undergone

---

[40] *Sympoiesis* ("making with") is a term frequently used by Haraway. "Nothing makes itself," she argues, because "nothing is really autopoietic or self-organizing" (Haraway 2016: 58).

since then. I suspect that modernity's end-of-history rhetoric may not be that different from Choerilos's agony. From a rational perspective, there is no reason to expect that the modern concept of progress will have a greater long-term value than past ideologies it has superseded (Becker 1969: 16), an observation that could apply to modernity itself. Besides, let us remember that in relation to the Earth's deep history, human history would "fill one-fifth of the last second of the last hour" (Benjamin 1999: 255). Or, as Westling puts it, we have "not been a factor in most of the history of planetary life; the Anthropocene could be seen as an unfortunate blip" (Westling 2022: 2).

To think of modernity as the end of history, a model to be repeated eternally, will in all probability be humanity's greatest hubris and most frantic delusion. We Moderns, the earth eaters, may err no less in our assumptions about the inevitability and superiority of our historical path, about boundless progress and infinite newness, than those cartographers who painstakingly drew the borders of their ecumene under the burning candles of antiquity. The ecological crisis has already made modernity look less like Hebe and more like that ageing portrait of Dorian Gray. History has always lurked around the corner, and it always will. Both actors and spectators are now requested to exit the play; it is time we rid ourselves of modernity's double coloniality, learned to unlearn, and decolonized our knowledge systems and our way of thinking about more-than-humans and human others like Byzantium. We must move beyond modernity. Tomorrow's newly yoked chariots should be driven on paths other than ours. The next modernity will have to be the real *post*-modernity – though, preferably, under a different name.

References

Abram, David (1996): *The Spell of the Sensuous: Perception and Language in a More-than-Human World*. New York, Vintage Books, 1997.

Académie Française (2005): *Dictionnaire de l'Académie Française* vol. 1. Paris, Fayard, Imprimerie Nationale.

Adorno, Theodor W. (2006): *History and Freedom: Lectures 1964–1965*. Ed. Rolf Tiedemann, trans. Rodney Livingstone. Cambridge, Polity.

Agapitos, Panagiotis (1992): "Byzantine Literature and Greek Philologists in the Nineteenth Century." *Classica et Mediaevalia* 43: 231–260.

Agapitos, Panagiotis (2003): "Ancient Models and Novel Mixtures: The Concept of Genre in Byzantine Funerary Literature from Photios to Eustathios of Thessalonike," in *Modern Greek Literature: Critical Essays*. Ed. Gregory Nagy and Anna Stavrakopoulou. New York, Routledge: 5–22.

Agapitos, Panagiotis (2015): "New Genres in the Twelfth Century: The *Schedourgia* of Theodore Prodromos." *Medioevo Greco* 15: 1–41.

Aguilar-Moreno, Manuel (2007): *Handbook to Life in the Aztec World*. New York, Oxford University Press.

Alcoff, Linda Martín (1996): *Real Knowing: New Versions of the Coherence Theory*. Ithaca, NY, Cornell University Press.

Alimonda, Héctor (2011): "La colonialidad de la naturaleza: una aproximación a la Ecología Política Latinoamericana," in *La naturaleza colonizada: ecología, política y minería en América Latina*. Ed. Héctor Alimonda. Buenos Aires, CLACSO: 21–58.

Allen, Amy (2017): *The End of Progress: Decolonizing the Normative Foundations of Critical Theory*. New York, Columbia University Press.

Anastos, Milton V. (1952): "Pletho, Strabo, and Columbus." *Annuaire de l'Institut de Philologie et d'Histoire Orientales et Slaves* xii: 1–18.

Anastos, Milton V. (1962): "The History of Byzantine Science." Report on the Dumbarton Oaks Symposium of 1961. *Dumbarton Oaks Papers* 16: 409–411.

Angelov, Dimiter G. (2003): "Byzantinism: The Imaginary and Real Heritage of Byzantium in Southeastern Europe," in *New Approaches to Balkan Studies*. Ed. Dimitris Keridis, Ellen Elias-Bursać, and Nicholas Yatromanolakis. Dulles, VA, Brassey's: 3–23.

Apffel-Marglin, Frédérique (2011): *Subversive Spiritualities: How Rituals Enact the World*. New York, Oxford University Press.

Apffel-Marglin, Frédérique (2012): "Development or Bio-Cultural Regeneration? Toward a Cosmocentric Economy." Keynote Address. *Development Dialogue Conference*, Institute of Social Studies, The Hague, October 8: 1–20.

Armstrong, Jeannette (2018): "A Single Strand: The Nsyilxcin Speaking People's *Tmix^w* Knowledge as a Model for Sustaining a Life-Force Place," in *Traditional Ecological Knowledge: Learning from Indigenous Practices for Environmental Sustainability*. Ed. Melissa K. Nelson and Dan Shilling. Cambridge, Cambridge University Press: 95–108.

Bacon, Francis (2011): *The Works of Francis Bacon, Volume 3: Philosophical Works 3*. Ed. James Spedding, Robert Leslie Ellis, and Douglas Denon Heath. New York, Cambridge University Press.

Barber, Marcus (2018): "Indigenous Knowledge, History and Environmental Change as Seen by Yolngu People of Blue Mud Bay, Northern Australia," in *Indigenous Knowledge for Climate Change Assessment and Adaptation*. Local & Indigenous Knowledge 2. Ed. Douglas Nakashima, Igor Krupnik, and Jennifer T. Rubis. Cambridge and Paris, Cambridge University Press and UNESCO: 106–122.

Bastien, Joseph W. (1982): "Exchange between Andean and Western Medicine." *Social Science and Medicine* 16, no. 7: 795–803.

Baucom, Ian (2014): "History 4°: Postcolonial Method and Anthropocene Time." *Cambridge Journal of Postcolonial Literary Inquiry* 1, no. 1: 123–142.

Bauman, Zygmunt (2000): *Liquid Modernity*. Cambridge, Polity.

Becker, Carl L. (1969): "Progress," in *The Idea of Progress since the Renaissance*. Ed. W. Warren Wagar. New York, John Wiley: 9–18.

Benavides, Annick (2022): "Spiritual Mining: Augustinian Images of Extraction in Colonial Peru." *The Art Bulletin*, 104, no. 4: 46–69.

Benjamin, Walter (1999): *Illuminations*. Ed. and intro Hannah Arendt, trans. Harry Zohn. London, Pimlico.

Bennett, David (2016): *Medicine and Pharmacy in Byzantine Hospitals: A Study of the Extant Formularies*. London, Routledge.

Berdan, Frances F. (2014): *Aztec Archaeology and Ethnohistory*. New York, Cambridge University Press.

Berressem, Hanjo (2009): "Structural Couplings: Radical Constructivism and a Deleuzian Ecologics," in *Deleuze/Guattari & Ecology*. Ed. Bernd Herzogenrath. Basingstoke, Palgrave Macmillan: 57–101.

Bodin, Helena (2016): "Whose Byzantinism – Ours or Theirs? On the Issue of Byzantinism from a Cultural Semiotic Perspective," in *The Reception of Byzantium in European Culture since 1500*. Ed. Przemysław Marciniak and Dion C. Smythe. Abingdon, Routledge: 11–42.

Bodin, Jean (1945): *Method for the Easy Comprehension of History*. Trans. Beatrice Reynolds. New York, Columbia University Press.

Boucher, Philip P. (1992): *Cannibal Encounters: Europeans and Island Caribs, 1492–1763*. Baltimore, The Johns Hopkins University Press.

Bouras-Vallianatos, Petros (2020): *Innovation in Byzantine Medicine: The Writings of John Zacharias Aktouarios (c.1275–c.1330)*. Oxford, Oxford University Press.

Braidotti, Rosi (2013): *The Posthuman*. Cambridge, Polity Press.

Bray, Warwick (1985): "Ancient American Metallurgy: Five Hundred Years of Study," in *The Art of Precolumbian Gold: The Jan Mitchell Collection*. Ed. Julie Jones. New York, Metropolitan Museum of Art: 76–84.

Brown, Marilyn A. and Benjamin K. Sovacool (2011): *Climate Change and Global Energy Security: Technology and Policy Options*. Cambridge, MA, MIT Press.

Browning, Robert (1995): "Tradition and Originality in Literary Criticism and Scholarship," in *Originality in Byzantine Literature, Art and Music: A Collection of Essays*. Ed. Antony Robert Littlewood. Oxford, Oxbow Books: 17–28.

Buffon, George-Louis Leclerc, comte de (1797): *Barr's Buffon. Buffon's Natural History* vol. IV. London, J. S. Barr.

Buringh, Eltjo (2011): *Medieval Manuscript Production in the Latin West: Explorations with a Global Database*. Leiden, Brill.

Cajete, Gregory (2018): "Native Science and Sustaining Indigenous Communities," in *Traditional Ecological Knowledge: Learning from Indigenous Practices for Environmental Sustainability*. Ed. Melissa K. Nelson and Dan Shilling. Cambridge, Cambridge University Press: 15–26.

Calderón de la Barca, Pedro (2005): *El gran teatro del mundo*. Ed. Enrique Rull Fernández. Barcelona, Debolsillo.

Calvino, Italo (1995): *Numbers in the Dark and Other Stories*. Trans. Tim Parks. New York, Penguin.

Cameron, Averil (2003): "Byzance dans le débat sur orientalisme," in *Byzance en Europe*. Ed. Marie-France Auzépy. Paris, Presses Universitaires de Vincennes: 235–250.

Cameron, Averil (2014): *Byzantine Matters*. Princeton, Princeton University Press.

Campbell, David A. (ed. and trans.) (1991): *Greek Lyric III: Stesichorus, Ibycus, Simonides, and Others*. Cambridge, MA, Harvard University Press.

Candiani, Vera S. (2014): *Dreaming of Dry Land: Environmental Transformation in Colonial Mexico City*. Stanford, CA, Stanford University Press.

Carlson, John B. (1975): "Lodestone Compass: Chinese or Olmec Primacy?" *Science, New Series* 189, no. 4205: 753–760.

Cilano, Cara and Elizabeth DeLoughrey (2007): "Against Authenticity: Global Knowledges and Postcolonial Ecocriticism." *Interdisciplinary Studies in Literature and Environment* 14, no. 1: 71–87.

Chakrabarty, Dipesh (2021): *The Climate of History in a Planetary Age.* Chicago, IL, University of Chicago Press.

Chapin III, F. Stuart, Steward T. A. Pickett, Mary E. Power, Robert B. Jackson, David M. Carter, and Clifford Duke (2011): "Earth Stewardship: A Strategy for Social-Ecological Transformation to Reverse Planetary Degradation." *Journal of Environmental Studies and Sciences* 1, no.1: 44–53.

Chroni, Maria (2010): "Θεραπείες ασθενειών με ζωϊκής προελεύσεως ύλες στα βυζαντινά ιατρικά κείμενα. Συμβολή στην μελέτη των αντιλήψεων για τις ασθένειες και τις θεραπείες τους στο Βυζάντιο." *Byzantina Symmeikta* 20: 143–194.

Clendinnen, Inga (1991): *Aztecs: An Interpretation.* New York, Cambridge University Press.

Clendinnen, Inga (2003): *Ambivalent Conquests: Maya and Spaniard in Yucatan, 1517–1570.* New York, Cambridge University Press.

Closs, Michael P. (1996): "A Survey of Aztec Numbers and Their Uses," in *Native American Mathematics.* Ed. Michael P. Closs. Austin, TX, University of Texas Press: 291–369.

Columbus, Christopher (1969): *The Four Voyages.* Ed. and trans. John M. Cohen. London, Penguin.

Comte, Auguste (1858): *The Positive Philosophy.* Trans. Harriet Martineau. New York, Calvin Blanchard.

Crutzen, Paul (2006): "Albedo Enhancement by Stratospheric Sulfur Injections: A Contribution to Resolve a Policy Dilemma?" *Climatic Change* 77: 211–219.

Crutzen, Paul and Eugene Stoermer (2000): "The Anthropocene." *Global Change Newsletter* 41: 16–17.

Cruz, Pablo (2006): "Mundos permeables y espacios peligrosos: consideraciones acerca de punkus y qaqas en el paisaje altoandino de Potosí, Bolivia." *Boletín del Museo Chileno de Arte Precolombino* 11, no. 2: 35–50.

Cummins, Thomas B. F. (2012): "Competing and Commensurate Values in Colonial Conditions: How They Are Expressed and Registered in the Sixteenth-Century Andes," in *The Construction of Value in the Ancient World.* Ed. John K. Papadopoulos and Gary Urton. Los Angeles, CA, Cotsen Institute of Archaeology Press: 406–423.

D'Altroy, Terence N. (2003): *The Incas.* Oxford, Blackwell.

Daly, Herman (1996): *Beyond Growth: The Economics of Sustainable Development.* Boston, MA, Beacon Press.

D'Ambrosio, Ubiratan (1977): "Science and Technology in Latin America during Its Discovery." *Impact of Science on Society* 27: 267–274.

Danowski, Déborah and Eduardo Viveiros de Castro (2017): *The Ends of the World*. Trans. Rodrigo Nunes. Cambridge, Polity.

Della Dora, Veronica (2016): *Landscape, Nature, and the Sacred in Byzantium*. Cambridge, Cambridge University Press.

de Mauro, Tullio (ed.) (2000): *Grande dizionario italiano dell' uso* vol. 1. Turin, Utet.

Descartes, René (2006): *A Discourse on the Method*. Trans. Ian Maclean. Oxford, Oxford University Press.

Descartes, René (2008): *Meditations on First Philosophy*. Trans., intro and notes Michael Moriarty. Oxford, Oxford University Press.

Devoto, Giacomo and Gian Carlo Oli (ed.) (1990): *Dizionario della lingua italiana*. Florence, Le Monnier.

Diderot, Denis and Jean le Rond d'Alembert (1779): *Encyclopédie ou diction-naire raisonné des sciences, des arts et des métiers* vol. 30. Geneva, Pellet.

Dodds, Eric Robertson (1973): *The Ancient Concept of Progress and Other Essays on Greek Literature and Belief*. Oxford, Clarendon Press.

Dreyfus, Hubert L. (1991): *Being-in-the-World: A Commentary on Heidegger's Being and Time, Division I*. Cambridge, MA, MIT Press.

Dussel, Enrique (1995): *The Invention of the Americas: Eclipse of "the Other" and the Myth of Modernity*. Trans. Michel D. Barber. New York, Continuum.

Dussel, Enrique (1996): *The Underside of Modernity: Apel, Ricœur, Rorty, Taylor, and the Philosophy of Liberation*. Trans. Eduardo Mendieta. New York, Humanity Books.

Dussel, Enrique (2000): "Europe, Modernity, and Eurocentrism." Trans. Javier Krauel and Virginia C. Tuma. *Nepantla: Views from the South* 1, no. 3: 465–478.

Dussel, Enrique (2002): "World-System and 'Trans'-Modernity." Trans. Alessandro Fornazzari. *Nepantla: Views from the South* 3, no. 2: 221–244.

El-Cheikh, Nadia Maria (2001): "Byzantium through the Islamic Prism from the Twelfth to the Thirteenth Century," in *The Crusades from the Perspective of Byzantium and the Muslim World*. Ed. Angeliki E. Laiou and Roy Parviz Mottahedeh. Washington, DC, Dumbarton Oaks Research Library and Collection: 53–69.

Escobar, Arturo (2003): "'Mundos y conocimientos de otro modo': el programa de investigación de modernidad/colonialidad latinoamericano." *Tabula Rasa* 1: 51–86.

Escobar, Arturo (2005): *Más allá del Tercer Mundo: globalización y diferencia*. Bogotá, Instituto Colombiano de Antropología e Historia.

Escobar, Arturo (2007): "Worlds and Knowledges Otherwise: The Latin American Modernity/Coloniality Research Program." *Cultural Studies* 21, no. 2–3: 179–210.

Escobar, Arturo (2011): "Epistemologías de la naturaleza y colonialidad de la naturaleza. Variedades de realismo y constructivismo," in *Cultura y Naturaleza: aproximaciones a propósito del bicentenario de la independencia de Colombia*. Ed. Leonardo Montenegro Martínez. Bogotá, Jardín Botánico José Celestino Mutis, Centro de Investigación y Desarrollo Científico: 50–72.

Finger, Stanley (1994): *Origins of Neuroscience: A History of Explorations into Brain Function*. New York, Oxford University Press.

Fontenelle, Bernard le Bovier de (1688): *Poésies pastorales de Monsieur de Fontenelle. Avec un traité sur la nature de l'églogue, et une digression sur les anciens et les modernes*. Paris, Michel Guérout.

Fontenelle, Bernard le Bovier de (1707): *Poésies pastorales. Avec un traité sur la nature de l'églogue, & une digression sur les anciens & les modernes*. London, Paul & Isaak Vaillant, Marchands Libraires.

Fontenelle, Bernard le Bovier de (1969): "Digression on the Ancients and the Moderns," in *The Idea of Progress since the Renaissance*. Ed. W. Warren Wagar. New York, John Wiley: 48–55.

Fontenelle, Bernard le Bovier de (1972): "Of the Origin of Fables," in *The Rise of Modern Mythology, 1680–1860*. Ed. and trans. Burton Feldman and Robert D. Richardson. Bloomington, IN, Indiana University Press: 10–18.

Foster, Lynn V. (2005): *Handbook to Life in the Ancient Maya World*. New York, Oxford University Press.

Fry, Roger (1996): "The Last Phase of Impressionism," in *A Roger Fry Reader*. Ed. Christopher Reed. Chicago, IL, Chicago University Press: 72–75.

Galeano, Eduardo (1971): *Las venas abiertas de América Latina*. Montevideo, Universidad de la República.

Gaukroger, Stephen (2001): *Francis Bacon and the Transformation of Early-Modern Philosophy*. New York, Cambridge University Press.

Geanakoplos, Deno John (1962): *Greek Scholars in Venice: Studies in the Dissemination of Greek Learning from Byzantium to Western Europe*. Cambridge, MA, Harvard University Press.

Geanakoplos, Deno John (1984): *Byzantium: Church, Society, and Civilization Seen through Contemporary Eyes*. Chicago, IL, University of Chicago Press.

Geanakoplos, Deno John (1993): *Μεσαιωνικός δυτικός πολιτισμός και οι κόσμοι του Βυζαντίου και του Ισλάμ*. Thessaloniki, Kyromanos Publications.

Gibbon, Edward (1997): *The History of the Decline and Fall of the Roman Empire* vol. V. London, Routledge/Thoemmes Press.

Giddens, Anthony (1991): *The Consequences of Modernity*. Cambridge, Polity.

Gilbert, Scott F., Jan Sapp, and Alfred I. Tauber (2012): "A Symbiotic View of Life: We Have Never Been Individuals." *Quarterly Review of Biology* 87, no. 4: 325–341.

Glick, Thomas E. (2013): "Islamic Technology," in *A Companion to the Philosophy of Technology*. Ed. Jan Kyrre Berg Olsen Friis, Stig Andur Pedersen, and Vincent F. Hendricks. Oxford, Wiley-Blackwell: 32–36.

Global Ocean Commission (2014): *From Decline to Recovery: A Rescue Package for the Global Ocean*. Somerville College, Oxford, Global Ocean Commission.

Goldwyn, Adam J. (2018): *Byzantine Ecocriticism: Women, Nature, and Power in the Medieval Greek Romance*. New York, Palgrave Macmillan.

Gombrich, Ernst Hans (1998): "Eastern Inventions and Western Response." *Daedalus* 127, no. 1: 193–205.

Guilbert, Louis, René Lagane, Georges Niobey et al. (1989): *Grand Larousse de la langue française* vol. 1. Paris, Librairie Larousse.

Guilland, Rodolphe (1926): *Essai sur Nicéphore Grégoras: l'homme et l'œuvre*. Paris, Librairie Orientaliste Paul Geuthner.

Haarer, Fiona (2010): "Writing Histories of Byzantium: The Historiography of Byzantine History," in *A Companion to Byzantium*. Ed. Liz James. Oxford, Wiley-Blackwell: 9–21.

Haas, Frans A. J. de (1996): *John Philoponus' New Definition of Prime Matter: Aspects of Its Background in Neoplatonism and Ancient Commentary Tradition*. Leiden, Brill.

Habermas, Jürgen (1979): *Communication and the Evolution of Society*. Trans. Thomas McCarthy. Boston, MA, Beacon Press.

Habermas, Jürgen (1981): "Modernity versus Postmodernity." Trans. Seyla Ben-Habib. *New German Critique* 22: 3–14.

Habermas, Jürgen (2010): "A Postsecular World Society? On the Philosophical Significance of Postsecular Consciousness and the Multicultural World Society." Interview with Eduardo Mendieta. *MRonline*, March 21, accessed on July 24, 2022, https://mronline.org/2010/03/21/a-postsecular-world-society-on-the-philo sophical-significance-of-postsecular-consciousness-and-the-multicultural-world-society/

Haraway, Donna J. (2016): *Staying with the Trouble: Making Kin in the Chthulucene*. Durham, NC, Duke University Press.

Hardoy, Jorge E. (1973): *Pre-Columbian Cities*. New York, Walker.

Harvey, Fiona (2022): "Humanity Faces 'Collective Suicide' Over Climate Crisis, Warns UN Chief." *The Guardian*, July 18.

Hegel, Georg Wilhelm Friedrich (2004): *The Philosophy of History*. Trans. and intro John Sibree. Mineola, NY, Dover Publications.

Heidegger, Martin (1982): *Basic Problems of Phenomenology*. Trans. and intro Albert Hofstadter. Bloomington, IN, Indiana University Press.

Hopkinson, Neil (ed.) (1999): *A Hellenistic Anthology*. Cambridge, Cambridge University Press.

Horden, Peregrine (2005): "How Medicalised Were Byzantine Hospitals?" *Medicina e Storia* 10: 45–74.

Huggan, Graham and Helen Tiffin (2015): *Postcolonial Ecocriticism: Literature, Animals, Environment*. Abingdon, Routlegde.

Ingold, Tim (1990): "An Anthropologist Looks at Biology." *Man* (N.S.) 25: 208–229.

Ioannides, Sakis (2022): "Από τη Δήλο στη Σελήνη για τη Γη: Μια νέα διεθνής πρωτοβουλία για το κλίμα και τον πολιτισμό." *Καθημερινή*, May 18, accessed on May 26, 2022, www.kathimerini.gr/culture/561864733/apo-ti-dilo-sti-selini-gia-ti-gi/

Iovino, Serenella (2021): *Italo Calvino's Animals*. Cambridge, Cambridge University Press.

IPCC (2014): *Climate Change 2014: Synthesis Report. Contribution of Working Groups I, II and III to the Fifth Assessment Report of the Intergovernmental Panel on Climate Change*. Geneva, IPCC.

IPCC (2021): *Climate Change 2021: The Physical Science Basis. Contribution of Working Group I to the Sixth Assessment Report of the Intergovernmental Panel on Climate Change*. Cambridge and New York, Cambridge University Press.

Jaenen, Cornelius J. (1982): "'Les Sauvages Ameriquains': Persistence into the 18th Century of Traditional French Concepts and Constructs for Comprehending Amerindians." *Ethnohistory* 29, no. 1: 43–56.

Jameson, Fredric (2002): *A Singular Modernity: Essay on the Ontology of the Present*. New York, Verso.

Jauss, Hans Robert (2005): "Modernity and Literary Tradition." Trans. Christian Thorne. *Critical Inquiry* 31, no. 2: 329–364.

Kaldellis, Anthony (2015): *The Byzantine Republic: People and Power in New Rome*. Cambridge, MA, Harvard University Press.

Kant, Immanuel (1784): "Idee zu einer allgemeinen Geschichte in weltbürgerlicher Absicht." *Berlinische Monatsschrift* (November), 385–411.

Kant, Immanuel (1891): "Idea for a Universal History from a Cosmopolitan Point of View," in *Principles of Politics*. Ed. and trans. William Hastie. Edinburgh, T. & T. Clark: 1–29.

Kant, Immanuel (1991): "An Answer to the Question: 'What Is Enlightenment'," in *Political Writings*. Ed. Hans Reiss. Cambridge, Cambridge University Press: 54–60.

Kaplan, Robert (2000): *The Nothing that Is: A Natural History of Zero*. New York, Oxford University Press.

Karkov, Nikolay and Jeffrey W. Robbins (2014): "Decoloniality and Crisis: Introduction." *Journal for Cultural and Religious Theory* 13, no.1: 1–10.

Kazhdan, Alexander (1991): "University of Constantinople," in *The Oxford Dictionary of Byzantium* vol. 3. Ed. Alexander P. Kazhdan, Alice-Mary Talbot, Anthony Cutler, Timothy E. Gregory, and Nancy P. Ševčenko. New York, Oxford University Press: 2143.

Kazhdan, Alexander (1995): "Innovation in Byzantium," in *Originality in Byzantine Literature, Art and Music: A Collection of Essays*. Ed. Antony Robert Littlewood. Oxford, Oxbow Books: 1–14.

Kefala, Eleni (2006): *Peripheral (Post) Modernity: The Syncretist Aesthetics of Borges, Piglia, Kalokyris, and Kyriakidis*. New York, Peter Lang.

Kefala, Eleni (2011): "Introduction," in *Negotiating Difference in the Hispanic World: From Conquest to Globalisation*. Ed. Eleni Kefala. Oxford, Wiley-Blackwell: 1–27.

Kefala, Eleni (2020): *The Conquered: Byzantium and America on the Cusp of Modernity*. Washington, DC, Dumbarton Oaks Research Library and Collection.

Kefala, Eleni (2022): *Buenos Aires Across the Arts: Five and One Theses on Modernity, 1921–1939*. Pittsburgh, PA, University of Pittsburgh Press.

Klein, Naomi (2015): *This Changes Everything: Capitalism vs the Climate*. London, Penguin.

Kolias, Taxiarchis (2005): "Τεχνολογία και πόλεμος στο Βυζάντιο." *Αρχαιολογία & Τέχνες* 96: 18–22.

Kopenawa, Davi and Bruce Albert (2013): *Falling Sky: Words of a Yanomami Shaman*. Trans. Nicholas Elliott and Alison Dundy. Cambridge, MA, Belknap Press.

Koselleck, Reinhart (2002): *The Practice of Conceptual History: Timing History, Spacing Concepts*. Trans. Todd Samuel Presner, Kerstin Behnke, Jobst Welge, and Adelheis Baker. Stanford, CA, Stanford University Press.

Krenak, Ailton (2020): *Ideas to Postpone the End of the World*. Trans. Anthony Doyle. Toronto, House of Anansi Press.

Krupnik, Igor, Jennifer T. Rubis, and Douglas Nakashima (2018): "Indigenous Knowledge for Climate Change Assessment and Adaptation: Epilogue," in *Indigenous Knowledge for Climate Change Assessment and Adaptation*. Local & Indigenous Knowledge 2. Ed. Douglas Nakashima, Igor Krupnik, and Jennifer T. Rubis. Cambridge and Paris, Cambridge University Press and UNESCO: 280–290.

Kureethadam, Joshtrom Isaac (2017): *The Philosophical Roots of the Ecological Crisis: Descartes and the Modern Worldview.* Newcastle, Cambridge Scholars.

Kurzweil, Ray (2005): *The Singularity Is Near: When Humans Transcend Biology.* New York, Viking.

Kusch, Rodolfo (2010): *Indigenous and Popular Thinking in America.* Trans. María Lugones and Joshua M. Price. Durham, NC, Duke University Press.

Lander, Edgardo (ed.) (2000): *La colonialidad del saber: eurocentrismo y ciencias sociales. Perspectivas latinoamericanas.* Buenos Aires, CLACSO.

Lander, Edgardo (2002): "La utopía del mercado total y el poder imperial." *Revista Venezolana de Economía y Ciencias Sociales* 8, no. 2: 51–79.

Langslow, David (2013): "Alexander of Tralles," in *The Encyclopedia of Ancient History.* Ed. Roger S. Bagnall, Kai Brodersen, Craige B. Champion, Andrew Erskine, and Sabine R. Huebner. Oxford, Blackwell: 305.

Larson, Carolyne R. (2020a): "Introduction: Tracing the Battle for History," in *The Conquest of the Desert: Argentina's Indigenous Peoples and the Battle for History.* Ed. Carolyne R. Larson. Albuquerque, NM, University of New Mexico: 1–16.

Larson, Carolyne R. (2020b): "The Conquest of the Desert: The Official Story," in *The Conquest of the Desert: Argentina's Indigenous Peoples and the Battle for History.* Ed. Carolyne R. Larson. Albuquerque, NM, University of New Mexico: 17–42.

Latour, Bruno (1993): *We Have Never Been Modern.* Trans. Catherine Porter. Cambridge, MA, Harvard University Press.

Latour, Bruno (2013): *An Inquiry into Modes of Existence: An Anthropology of the Moderns.* Trans. Catherine Porter. Cambridge, MA, Harvard University Press.

Latour, Bruno (2017): *Facing Gaia: Eight Lectures on the New Climatic Regime.* Trans. Catherine Porter. Cambridge, Polity.

Latour, Bruno (2018): *Down to Earth: Politics in the New Climatic Regime.* Trans. Catherine Porter. Cambridge, Polity.

Latour, Bruno (2021): *After Lockdown: A Metamorphosis.* Trans. Julie Rose. Cambridge, Polity.

Lazaris, Stavros (ed.) (2020a): *A Companion to Byzantine Science.* Leiden, Brill.

Lazaris, Stavros (2020b): "Introduction," in *A Companion to Byzantine Science.* Ed. Stavros Lazaris. Leiden, Brill: 1–26.

Lazaris, Stavros (2020c): "Veterinary Medicine," in *A Companion to Byzantine Science.* Ed. Stavros Lazaris. Leiden, Brill: 404–428.

Lecky, William (1869): *History of European Morals: From Augustus to Charlemagne* vol. 2. New York, D. Appleton.

Lefebvre, Henri (1995): "What Is Modernity?" in *Introduction to Modernity: Twelve Preludes, September 1959–May 1961*. Trans. John Moore. London, Verso: 168–237.

Lemerle, Paul (1986): *Byzantine Humanism, the First Phase: Notes and Remarks on Education and Culture in Byzantium from Its Origins to the 10th Century*. Trans. Helen Lindsay and Ann Moffatt. Canberra, Australian Association for Byzantine Studies.

Lenton, Tim (2016): *Earth System Science: A Very Short Introduction*. Oxford, Oxford University Press.

León-Portilla, Miguel (1963): *Aztec Thought and Culture: A Study of the Ancient Nahuatl Mind*. Trans. Jack Emory Davis. Norman, OK, University of Oklahoma Press.

Leopold, Aldo (2001): *A Sand County Almanac: With Essays on Conservation*. New York: Oxford University Press.

Littlewood, Antony Robert (ed.) (1995): *Originality in Byzantine Literature, Art and Music: A Collection of Essays*. Oxford, Oxbow Books.

López Austin, Alfredo and Leonardo López Luján (2001): *Mexico's Indigenous Past*. Trans. Bernard R. Ortiz de Montellano. Norman, OK, University of Oklahoma Press.

Lovejoy, Shaun (2019): *Weather, Macroweather, and the Climate: Our Random Yet Predictable Atmosphere*. New York, Oxford University Press.

Lovelock, James (1995): *The Ages of Gaia: A Biography of Our Living Earth*. New York, Norton.

Lyotard, Jean-François (1984): *The Postmodern Condition: A Report on Knowledge*. Trans. Geoff Bennington and Brian Massumi. Manchester, Manchester University Press.

MacGregor, Neil (2011): *A History of the World in 100 Objects*. London, Allen Lane.

Magdalino, Paul (2013): "Byzantine Encyclopaedism of the Ninth and Tenth Centuries," in *Encyclopaedism from Antiquity to the Renaissance*. Ed. Jason König and Greg Woolf. Cambridge, Cambridge University Press: 219–231.

Maldonado-Torres, Nelson (2007): "Sobre la colonialidad del ser: contribuciones al desarrollo de un concepto," in *El giro decolonial: reflexiones para una diversidad epistémica más allá del capitalismo global*. Ed. Santiago Castro-Gómez and Ramón Grosfoguel. Bogotá, Iesco-Pensar-Siglo del Hombre Editores: 127–167.

Malmström, Vincent H. (2008): "Magnetism in Mesoamerica," in *Encyclopaedia of the History of Science, Technology, and Medicine in Non-Western Cultures*. Ed. Helaine Selin. New York, Springer: 1265–1267.

Malpass, Michael A. (2009): *Daily Life in the Inca Empire*. Westport, CT, Greenwood Press.

Maran, Timo (2020): *Ecosemiotics: The Study of Signs in Changing Ecologies*. Cambridge, Cambridge University Press.

Marciniak, Przemysław (2018): "Oriental Like Byzantium: Some Remarks on Similarities between Byzantinism and Orientalism," in *Imagining Byzantium: Perceptions, Patterns, Problems*. Ed. Alena Alshanskaya, Andreas Gietzen, and Christina Hadjiafxenti. Mainz, Verlag des Römisch-Germanischen Zentralmuseums: 47–54.

Marcuse, Herbert (2002): *One-Dimensional Man: Studies in the Ideology of Advanced Industrial Society*. London, Routledge.

Markey, Lia (2012): "Stradano's Allegorical Invention of the Americas in Late Sixteenth-Century Florence." *Renaissance Quarterly* 65, no. 2: 385–442.

Markopoulos, Athanasios (2008): "Education," in *The Oxford Handbook of Byzantine Studies*. Ed. Robin Cormack, John F. Haldon, and Elizabeth Jeffreys. Oxford, Oxford University Press: 785–795.

Martinez, Dennis (2018): "Redefining Sustainability through Kincentric Ecology: Reclaiming Indigenous Lands, Knowledge, and Ethics," in *Traditional Ecological Knowledge: Learning from Indigenous Practices for Environmental Sustainability*. Ed. Melissa K. Nelson and Dan Shilling. Cambridge, Cambridge University Press: 139–174.

Marx, Karl and Friedrich Engels (1980): "Speech at the Anniversary of *The People's Paper*," in *Collected Works* vol. 14. Ed. Jack Cohen, Maurice Cornforth, Maurice Dobb et al. London, Lawrence & Wishart, 655–656.

Mavroudi, Maria (2013): "Byzantine Science," in *The Encyclopedia of Ancient History*. Ed. Roger S. Bagnall, Kai Brodersen, Craige B. Champion, Andrew Erskine, and Sabine R. Huebner. Oxford, Blackwell: 6063–6065.

Mavroudi, Maria (2015): "Translations from Greek into Arabic and Latin during the Middle Ages: Searching for the Classical Tradition." *Speculum* 90, no. 1: 28–59.

Mavroudi, Maria (2024): "Arabic Terms in Byzantine *Materia Medica*: Oral and Textual Transmission," in *Drugs in the Medieval Mediterranean: Transmission and Circulation of Pharmacological Knowledge*. Ed. Petros Bouras-Vallianatos and Dionysios Stathakopoulos. Cambridge, Cambridge University Press: 130–183.

Mayor, Adrienne (2013): "Greek Fire," in *The Encyclopedia of Ancient History*. Ed. Roger S. Bagnall, Kai Brodersen, Craige B. Champion, Andrew Erskine, and Sabine R. Huebner. Oxford, Blackwell: 2984–2985.

McCabe, Anne (2007): *A Byzantine Encyclopaedia of Horse Medicine: The Sources, Compilation, and Transmission of the Hippiatrica*. Oxford, Oxford University Press.

McGeer, Eric (1991): "Greek Fire," in *The Oxford Dictionary of Byzantium* vol. 2. Ed. Alexander P. Kazhdan, Alice-Mary Talbot, Anthony Cutler, Timothy E. Gregory, and Nancy P. Ševčenko. New York, Oxford University Press: 873.

McNeill, John Robert and Peter Engelke (2014): *The Great Acceleration: An Environmental History of the Anthropocene since 1945*. Cambridge, MA, Belknap Press.

Mendoza, Ruben G. (1997): "Metallurgy in Meso and North America," in *Encyclopaedia of the History of Science, Technology, and Medicine in Non-western Cultures*. Ed. Helaine Selin. Dordrecht, Kluwer Academic: 730–733.

Mendoza, Ruben G. (2003): "Lords of the Medicine Bag: Medical Science and Traditional Practice in Ancient Peru and South America," in *Medicine across Cultures: History and Practice of Medicine in Non-Western Cultures*. Ed. Helaine Selin. Boston, MA, Kluwer Academic: 225–257.

Michelis, Panayotis A. (1955): *An Aesthetic Approach to Byzantine Art*. London, B. T. Batsford.

Mignolo, Walter (1995): *The Darker Side of the Renaissance: Literacy, Territoriality and Colonization*. Ann Arbor, MI, The University of Michigan Press.

Mignolo, Walter (2001): "Introducción," in *Capitalismo y geopolítica del conocimiento: el eurocentrismo y la filosofía de la liberación en el debate intelectual contemporáneo*. Ed. Walter Mignolo. Buenos Aires, Ediciones del Signo: 9–53.

Mignolo, Walter (2007): "Delinking: The Rhetoric of Modernity, the Logic of Coloniality and the Grammar of De-Coloniality." *Cultural Studies* 21, no. 2: 449–514.

Miller, Timothy S. (1997): *The Birth of the Hospital in the Byzantine Empire*. Baltimore, MD, The Johns Hopkins University Press.

Mitrović, Branko (2004): "Leon Battista Alberti and the Homogeneity of Space." *Journal of the Society of Architectural Historians* 63, no. 4: 424–439.

Mondragón, Carlos (2018): "Forest, Reef and Sea-Level Rise in North Vanuatu: Seasonal Environmental Practices and Climate Fluctuations in Island Melanesia," in *Indigenous Knowledge for Climate Change Assessment and Adaptation*. Local & Indigenous Knowledge 2. Ed. Douglas Nakashima, Igor Krupnik, and Jennifer T. Rubis. Cambridge and Paris, Cambridge University Press and UNESCO: 23–40.

Montana, Fausto (2011): "Dallo scaffale mediceo della poesia greca antica," in *Voci dell'oriente: miniature e testi classici da Bisanzio alla Biblioteca Medicea Laurenziana*. Ed. Massimo Bernabò. Florence, Edizioni Polistampa: 37–46.

Moore, Jason W. (2017): "The Capitalocene, Part I: On the Nature and Origins of Our Ecological Crisis." *The Journal of Peasant Studies* 44, no. 3: 594–630.

Mundy, Barbara E. (2015): *The Death of Aztec Tenochtitlan, the Life of Mexico City*. Austin, TX, University of Texas Press.

Mylonas, Anastasios I., Effie Poulakou-Rebelakou, and Evangelia Ch. Papadopoulou (2015): "The Evolution of Pediatric Oral, Maxillofacial, and Craniofacial Surgery, from Hippocrates the Koan to Paul Tessier: A Brief Historical Review." *Hellenic Archives of Oral & Maxillofacial Surgery* 16, no. 3: 103–118.

Nakashima, Douglas, Jennifer T. Rubis, and Igor Krupnik (2018): "Indigenous Knowledge for Climate Change Assessment and Adaptation: Introduction," in *Indigenous Knowledge for Climate Change Assessment and Adaptation*. Local & Indigenous Knowledge 2. Ed. Douglas Nakashima, Igor Krupnik, and Jennifer T. Rubis. Cambridge and Paris, Cambridge University Press and UNESCO: 1–20.

Needham, Joseph (2000): *Science and Civilization in China* vol. IV. Cambridge, Cambridge University Press.

Nelson, Melissa K. (2018): "Conclusion: Back in Our Tracks – Embodying Kinship as If the Future Mattered," in *Traditional Ecological Knowledge: Learning from Indigenous Practices for Environmental Sustainability*. Ed. Melissa K. Nelson and Dan Shilling. Cambridge, Cambridge University Press: 250–266.

Nelson, Robert S. (1995): "The Italian Appreciation and Appropriation of Illuminated Byzantine Manuscripts, ca. 1200–1450." *Dumbarton Oaks Papers* 49 (Symposium on Byzantium and the Italians, 13th–15th Centuries): 209–235.

Nelson, Robert S. (2004a): "Byzantium and the Rebirth of Art and Learning in Italy and France," in *Byzantium: Faith and Power (1261–1557)*. Ed. Helen C. Evans. New York, Metropolitan Museum of Art: 515–523.

Nelson, Robert S. (2004b): "The *Dynameron* of Nicholas Myrepsos and Other Medical Texts," in *Byzantium: Faith and Power (1261–1557)*. Ed. Helen C. Evans. New York, Metropolitan Museum of Art: 526.

Nelson, Robert S. (2015): "Modernism's Byzantium, Byzantium's Modernism," in *Byzantium/Modernism: The Byzantine as Method in Modernity*. Ed. Roland Betancourt and Maria Taroutina. Leiden, Brill: 15–36.

Nielsen, Keld (2013): "Western Technology," in *A Companion to the Philosophy of Technology*. Ed. Jan Kyrre Berg Olsen Friis, Stig Andur Pedersen, and Vincent F. Hendricks. Oxford, Blackwell: 23–27.

Nowlin, Christopher (2021): "Indigenous Capitalism and Resource Development in an Age of Climate Change." *McGill Journal of Sustainable Development Law / Revue de droit du développement durable de McGill* 17, no. 1: 71–97.

Oberhelman, Steven M. (2013): "Paul of Aigina," in *The Encyclopedia of Ancient History*. Ed. Roger S. Bagnall, Kai Brodersen, Craige B. Champion, Andrew Erskine, and Sabine R. Huebner. Oxford, Blackwell: 5101–5102.

Oldmeadow, Peter (2010): *Religion and Retributive Logic: Essays in Honour of Professor Garry W. Trompf*. Ed. Carole M. Cusack and Christopher Hartney. Leiden, Brill: 267–287.

Ortiz de Montellano, Bernard R. (1990): *Aztec Medicine, Health, and Nutrition*. New Brunswick, NJ, Rutgers University Press.

Ousterhout, Robert (2015): "Byzantine Architecture: A Moving Target?" in *Byzantium/Modernism: The Byzantine as Method in Modernity*. Ed. Roland Betancourt and Maria Taroutina. Leiden, Brill: 163–176.

Owen, David S. (2002): *Between Reason and History: Habermas and the Idea of Progress*. Albany, NY, SUNY Press.

Oxfam (2022): *Inequality Kills: The Unparalleled Action Needed to Combat Unprecedented Inequality in the Wake of COVID-19*. Oxford, Oxfam International.

Papadakis, Marios, Evangelos Sfakiotakis, Marios Fragakis et al. (2014): "Plastic Surgery of the Face in Byzantine Times," in *Medicine and Healing in the Ancient Mediterranean World*. Ed. Demetrios Michaelides. Oxford, Oxbow Books: 155–162.

Papadakis, Marios, Eelco de Bree, Constantinos Trompoukis, and Andreas Manios (2015): "Management of Penile Tumours during the Byzantine Period." *JBUON* 20, no. 2: 653–657.

Pennock, Caroline Dodds (2013): "'A Remarkably Patterned Life': Domestic and Public in the Aztec Household City," in *Gender and the City before Modernity*. Ed. Lin Foxhall and Gabriele Neher. Oxford, Wiley and Blackwell: 38–56.

Pentogalos, Gerasimos and Ioannis Lascaratos (1984): "A Surgical Operation on Siamese Twins during the Tenth Century in Byzantium." *Bulletin of the History of Medicine* 58: 99–102.

Pérez Martín, Inmaculada and Divna Manolova (2020): "Science Teaching and Learning Methods in Byzantium," in *A Companion to Byzantine Science*. Ed. Stavros Lazaris. Leiden, Brill: 53–104.

Plumwood, Val (2003): "Decolonizing Relationships with Nature," in *Decolonizing Nature: Strategies for Conservation in a Post-Colonial Era*. Ed. William M. Adams and Martin Mulligan. London: Earthscan, 51–78.

Poulakou-Rebelakou, Effie (2000): "Pediatric Practice during Byzantine Times." *Archives of Hellenic Medicine* 17, no. 3: 326–331.

Poulakou-Rebelakou, Effie, Marianne Karamanou, and George Androutsos (2011): "Urological Diseases of the Byzantine Emperors (330–1453)." *Urology* 77, no. 2: 269–273.

Prioreschi, Plinio (2002): "The Idea of Scientific Progress in Antiquity and in the Middle Ages." *Vesalius* VIII, no. 1: 34–45.

Purdy, Jedediah (2015): *After Nature: A Politics of the Anthropocene.* Cambridge, MA, Harvard University Press.

Quijano, Aníbal (2000): "Colonialidad del poder y clasificación social." *Journal of World-System Research* 6, no. 2: 342–386.

Real Academia Española (2014): *Diccionario de la lengua española.* Madrid, Espasa Calpe.

Ritzer, George and Allan Liska (1997): "'McDisneyization' and 'Post-Tourism': Complementary Perspectives on Contemporary Tourism," in *Touring Cultures: Transformations of Travel and Theory.* Ed. Chris Rojek and John Urry. London, Routledge: 96–109.

Robert, Paul, Josette Rey-Debove, and Alain Rey (2012): *Le Petit Robert.* Paris, Le Robert.

Rodhe, Henning, Robert Charlson, and Elizabeth Crawford (1997): "Svante Arrhenius and the Greenhouse Effect." *Ambio* 26, no. 1: 2–5.

Ruddiman, William F. (2013): "The Anthropocene." *Annual Review of Earth and Planetary Sciences* 41: 45–68.

Said, Edward (1979): *Orientalism.* New York, Vintage Books.

Said, Edward (1994): *Culture and Imperialism.* London, Vintage Books.

Salmon, Enrique (2000): "Kincentric Ecology: Indigenous Perceptions of the Human-Nature Relationship." *Ecological Applications* 10, no. 5: 1327–1332.

Salmon, Thomas (2020): "The Byzantine Science of Warfare: From Treatises to Battlefield," in *A Companion to Byzantine Science.* Ed. Stavros Lazaris. Leiden, Brill: 429–463.

Sarewitz, Daniel (2013): "The Idea of Progress," in *A Companion to the Philosophy of Technology.* Ed. Jan Kyrre Berg Olsen Friis, Stig Andur Pedersen, and Vincent F. Hendricks. Oxford, Wiley-Blackwell: 303–307.

Sarmiento, Domingo Faustino (2001): *Facundo: civilización y barbarie.* Buenos Aires, Altamira.

Scarborough, John (1997): "The Life and Times of Alexander of Tralles." *Expedition* 39, no. 2: 51–60.

Scarborough, John and Anthony Cutler (1991): "Hippiatrica," in *The Oxford Dictionary of Byzantium* vol. 2. Ed. Alexander P. Kazhdan, Alice-Mary Talbot, Anthony Cutler, Timothy E. Gregory, and Nancy P. Ševčenko. New York, Oxford University Press: 933–934.

Schell, Jonathan (1982): "The Fate of the Earth: A Republic of Insects and Grass." *New Yorker* 58, 47–113.

Schell, Jonathan (2000): *The Fate of the Earth and The Abolition*. Stanford, CA, Stanford University Press.

Schlobach, Jochen (2013): "Quarrel of the Ancients and the Moderns," in *Encyclopedia of the Enlightenment* vol. 1. Ed. Michel Delon. London and New York, Routledge: 64–70.

Scholze-Stubenrecht, Werner et al. (ed.) (1999): *Duden: das große Wörterbuch der deutschen Sprache* vol. 2. Mannheim, Dudenverlag.

Sen, Amartya (2001): *Development as Freedom*. New York, Oxford University Press.

Shakespeare, William (2004): *As You Like It: A Comedy*. Ed. Barbara A. Mowat and Paul Werstine. New York, Washington Square Press.

Shilling, Dan (2018): "Introduction: The Soul of Sustainability," in *Traditional Ecological Knowledge: Learning from Indigenous Practices for Environmental Sustainability*. Ed. Melissa K. Nelson and Dan Shilling. Cambridge, Cambridge University Press: 3–14.

Smith, Pamela H. (2006): "Art, Science, and Visual Culture in Early Modern Europe." *Isis* 97, no. 1: 83–100.

Soucek, Priscilla (1997): "Byzantium and the Islamic East," in *The Glory of Byzantium: Art and Culture of the Middle Byzantine Era, A.D. 843–1261*. Ed. Helen C. Evans and William D. Wixom. New York, Metropolitan Museum of Art: 403–411.

Sousa Santos, Boaventura de, João Arriscado Nunes, and Maria Paula Meneses (2008): "Introduction: Opening Up the Canon of Knowledge and Recognition of Difference," in *Another Knowledge Is Possible: Beyond Northern Epistemologies*. Ed. Boaventura de Sousa Santos. New York, Verso: xix–lxii.

Stamatopoulos, Dimitrios (2013): "From the *Vyzantism* of K. Leont'ev to the *Vyzantinism* of I. I. Sokolov: The Byzantine Orthodox East as a Motif of Russian Orientalism," in *Héritages de Byzance en Europe du Sud-Est à l'époque moderne et contemporaine*. Ed. Olivier Delouis, Anne Couderc, and Petre Guran. Athens, École Française d'Athènes: 321–340.

Stengers, Isabelle (2015): *In Catastrophic Times: Resisting the Coming Barbarism*. London, Open Humanities Press in collaboration with Meson Press.

Stevenson, Angus (ed.) (2010): *Oxford Dictionary of English*. Oxford, Oxford University Press.

Stouraitis, Yannis (2022): "Is Byzantinism an Orientalism? Reflections on Byzantium's Constructed Identities and Debated Ideologies," in *Identities and Ideologies in the Medieval East Roman World*. Ed. Yannis Stouraitis. Edinburgh, Edinburgh University Press: 19–47.

Sutton, Mark Q. and Eugene N. Anderson (2014): *Introduction to Cultural Ecology*. Lanham, MA, AltaMira Press.

Syvitski, James, Jan Zalasiewicz, and Colin P. Summerhayes (2019): "Changes to Holocene/Anthropocene Patterns of Sedimentation from Terrestrial to Marine," in *The Anthropocene as a Geological Time Unit: A Guide to the Scientific Evidence and Current Debate*. Ed. Jan Zalasiewicz, Colin N. Waters, Mark Williams, and Colin P. Summerhayes. Cambridge, Cambridge University Press: 90–108.

Tannenbaum, Rebecca (2012): *Health and Wellness in Colonial America*. Santa Barbara, CA, ABC Clio.

Taroutina, Maria (2015): "Introduction: Byzantium and Modernism," in *Byzantium/Modernism: The Byzantine as Method in Modernity*. Ed. Roland Betancourt and Maria Taroutina. Leiden, Brill: 1–12.

Temkin, Owsei (1962): "Byzantine Medicine: Tradition and Empiricism." *Dumbarton Oaks Papers* 16: 97–115.

Tihon, Anne (2013): "Science in the Byzantine Empire," in *The Cambridge History of Science Volume 2: Medieval Science*. Ed. David C. Lindberg and Michael H. Shank. Cambridge, Cambridge University Press: 190–206.

Touwaide, Alain (2020): "Medicine and Pharmacy," in *A Companion to Byzantine Science*. Ed. Stavros Lazaris. Leiden, Brill: 354–403.

Traka, Diana (2007): "Η βυζαντινή ιατρική." *Αρχαιολογία & Τέχνες* 103: 6–9.

Treadgold, Warren T. (1984): "The Macedonian Renaissance," in *Renaissances before the Renaissance: Cultural Revivals of Late Antiquity and the Middle Ages*. Ed. Warren T. Treadgold. Stanford, CA, Stanford University Press: 75–98.

Turgot, Anne-Robert-Jacques (2018): *Œuvres de Turgot et documents le concernant* vol. 1. Ed. Gustave Schelle. Paris, Institut Coppet.

UNDP (2011): *Human Development Report – Sustainability and Equity: A Better Future for All*. New York, Palgrave Macmillan.

Varese, Stefano (2011): "El dilema antropocéntrico: notas sobre la economía política de la naturaleza en la cultura indígena." *Quaderns* 27: 97–122.

Vasiliev, Alexander Alexandrovich (1952): *History of the Byzantine Empire, 324–1453*. Madison, WI, The University of Wisconsin Press.

Verano, John W. (2016): *The Art and Archaeology of Trepanation in Ancient Peru*. Washington, DC, Dumbarton Oaks Research Library and Collection.

Verpeaux, Jean (1959): *Nicéphore Choumnos: Homme d'état et humaniste byzantin (ca. 1250/1255–1327)*. Paris, Éditions A. et J. Picard & Cie.

Viesca, Carlos (2003): "Medicine in Ancient Mesoamerica," in *Medicine across Cultures: History and Practice of Medicine in Non-Western Cultures*. Ed. Helaine Selin. Boston, MA, Kluwer Academic, 259–283.

Villani, Filippo (1847): *Liber de civitatis Florentiae famosis civibus*. Ed. Gustavo C. Galletti. Florence, Mazzoni.

Voltaire (2013): *Les Œuvres completes: Essai sur les mœurs et l'esprit des nations* vol. 26A. Oxford, Voltaire Foundation.

Wagar, W. Warren (ed.) (1969): *The Idea of Progress since the Renaissance*. New York, John Wiley.

Wagner, Peter (2022): "History 4°Celsius. Search for a Method in the Age of the Anthropocene; The Climate of History in a Planetary Age; Grand Transitions. How the Modern World Was Made." *The AAG Review of Books* 10, no. 1: 30–35.

Wahrig-Burfeind, Renate (ed.) (2000): *Wahrig Deutsches Wörterbuch* vol. 2. Gütersloh/Munich, Bertelsmann Lexikon Verlag.

Walsh, Catherine (2012): "Interculturalidad y (de)colonialidad: perspectivas críticas y políticas." *Visão Global* 15, no. 1–2: 61–74.

Westling, Louise (2022): *Deep History, Climate Change, and the Evolution of Human Culture*. Cambridge, Cambridge University Press.

White, Lynn (1996): "The Historical Roots of Our Ecologic Crisis," in *The Ecocriticism Reader: Landmarks in Literary Ecology*. Ed. Cheryll Glotfelty and Harold Fromm. Athens, GA, University of Georgia Press: 3–14.

Whyte, Kyle (2018): "What Do Indigenous Knowledges Do for Indigenous Peoples," in *Traditional Ecological Knowledge: Learning from Indigenous Practices for Environmental Sustainability*. Ed. Melissa K. Nelson and Dan Shilling. Cambridge, Cambridge University Press: 57–81.

Wilder-Smith, Annelies (2021): "COVID-19 in Comparison with Other Emerging Viral Diseases: Risk of Geographic Spread via Travel." *Tropical Diseases, Travel Medicine and Vaccines* 7, no. 3: 1–11.

Wixom, William D. (1997): "Byzantine Art and the Latin West," in *The Glory of Byzantium: Art and Culture of the Middle Byzantine Era, A.D. 843–1261*. Ed. Helen C. Evans and William D. Wixom. New York, Metropolitan Museum of Art: 435–449.

Wolfgramm, Rachel, Chellie Spiller, Carla Houkamau, and Manuka Henare (2018): "Home: Resistance, Resilience, and Innovation in Māori Economies of Well-Being," in *Traditional Ecological Knowledge: Learning from Indigenous Practices for Environmental Sustainability*. Ed. Melissa K. Nelson and Dan Shilling. Cambridge, Cambridge University Press: 213–228.

World Bank (2012): *Turn Down the Heat: Why a 4°C Warmer World Must Be Avoided*. Washington, DC, World Bank.

World Inequality Lab (2022): *World Inequality Report*. Paris, World Inequality Lab.

WWF (2020): *Stop Ghost Gear: The Most Deadly Form of Marine Plastic Debris*. Gland, World Wide Fund for Nature.

Zagklas, Nikos (2017): "Experimenting with Prose and Verse in Twelfth-Century Byzantium." *Dumbarton Oaks Papers* 71: 229–248.

Zagklas, Nikos (2018): "Metrical *Polyeideia* and Generic Innovation in the Twelfth Century: The Multimetric Cycles of Occasional Poetry," in *Middle and Late Byzantine Poetry: Texts and Contexts*. Ed. Andreas Rhoby and Nikos Zagklas. Turnhout, Brepols: 43–70.

Zeller, Jules (1871): *Entretiens sur l'histoire: Antiquité et Moyen Âge* vol. I. Paris, Didier et Cie, Libraires-Éditeurs.

Žižek, Slavoj (2010): *Living in the End of Times*. New York, Verso.

Cambridge Elements ≡

Environmental Humanities

Louise Westling

University of Oregon

Louise Westling is an American scholar of literature and environmental humanities who was a founding member of the Association for the Study of Literature and Environment and its President in 1998. She has been active in the international movement for environmental cultural studies, teaching and writing on landscape imagery in literature, critical animal studies, biosemiotics, phenomenology, and deep history.

Serenella Iovino

University of North Carolina at Chapel Hill

Serenella Iovino is Professor of Italian Studies and Environmental Humanities at the University of North Carolina at Chapel Hill. She has written on a wide range of topics, including environmental ethics and ecocritical theory, bioregionalism and landscape studies, ecofeminism and posthumanism, comparative literature, eco-art, and the Anthropocene.

Timo Maran

University of Tartu

Timo Maran is an Estonian semiotician and poet. Maran is Professor of Ecosemiotics and Environmental Humanities and Head of the Department of Semiotics at the University of Tartu. His research interests are semiotic relations of nature and culture, Estonian nature writing, zoosemiotics and species conservation, and semiotics of biological mimicry.

About the Series

The environmental humanities is a new transdisciplinary complex of approaches to the embeddedness of human life and culture in all the dynamics that characterize the life of the planet. These approaches reexamine our species' history in light of the intensifying awareness of drastic climate change and ongoing mass extinction. To engage this reality, Cambridge Elements in Environmental Humanities builds on the idea of a more hybrid and participatory mode of research and debate, connecting critical and creative fields.

Cambridge Elements ☰

Environmental Humanities

Elements in the Series

A full series listing is available at: www.cambridge.org/EIEH

Printed in the United States
by Baker & Taylor Publisher Services